BLIND FREDDY

For many years Adrian Mitchell taught Australian literature, first at the University of Adelaide, and subsequently at the University of Sydney. On retirement, especially relishing the ironies inherent in Australian history, he has turned to writing a series of books that are all biographical in one form or another and all published by Wakefield Press. His *Plein Airs and Graces: The life and times of George Collingridge* was shortlisted for the Prime Minister's Literary Award.

BY THE SAME AUTHOR

Where Shadows Have Fallen: The descent of Henry Kendall

The Profilist: The notebooks of Ethan Dibble

The Beachcomber's Wife

Plein Airs and Graces: The life and times of George Collingridge

Peat Island: Dreaming and desecration

From Corner to Corner: The line of Henry Colless

Drawing the Crow

Dampier's Monkey: The south seas voyages of William Dampier

BLIND FREDDY

The Pottinger Attainment

ADRIAN MITCHELL

Wakefield Press

Wakefield Press
16 Rose Street
Mile End
South Australia 5031
www.wakefieldpress.com.au

First published 2026

Edited by Penelope Curtin, Wakefield Press
Book design and typesetting by Duncan Blachford, Typography Studio

ISBN 978 1 92338 866 6

A catalogue record for this book is available from the National Library of Australia

Wakefield Press thanks Coriole Vineyards for their continued support

Some are born great, some achieve greatness,
and some have greatness thrust upon them.

—WILLIAM SHAKESPEARE, *Twelfth Night*

CONTENTS

ACKNOWLEDGEMENTS

THIS BOOK BEGAN as one of those Covid projects that whiled away the tedium of those sequestered times, when it seemed much more agreeable to keep one's own company for a bit. Alright, inevitable too.

But once wind of this project started wafting about, various friends and acquaintances made a move – preserving the recommended distance, slightly beyond elbow contact – to encourage me to get on with it. Among them, I thank the genteel Muff Nettleton for advice on how to come down from a high horse (is there any other sort?), and Rob Mayrick for insight into the layered inflections of Belfast. At a crucial stage Michael Bosher retrieved a lost draft of this text from the ether, when no traces were to be seen, let alone gathered up.

Early on I took advantage of Mark Matthews's omnibus website www.benhallaustralianbushranger.com and of course the resources of various libraries – the Fisher Library at the University of Sydney, the State Library of New South Wales, the National Library of Australia (hurrah for the treasures of their Trove), and not least the local history collections of the Forbes Library and the Orange Library, at a safe distance from any other reader. I am grateful for the assistance provided at each of those collections.

A copy editor is something like a patrol officer, it seems to me – one who steps out from behind cover and brings unseemly or irresponsible progress to a halt. Ignorance, she will say, is no defence; nor is wilfulness. That, she cautions, is not how to get brought to book. A copy editor's role is to ensure good order and the observation of established procedure. So my thanks once more to the irresistible Penelope Curtin, she of the thin blue line, and to Wakefield Press, for their assistance in bringing blinking Blind Freddy back into the light of day.

THE SADDLING PADDOCK

THE POTTINGERS WERE a family of considerable antiquity. They attached significant importance to that adornment, and they never forgot it. Not that very much was involved in magnifying it: all they had to do was to inherit their nominal patrimony. It grew by itself. How good is that?

Their family motto – *virtus in ardua* – might be understood as meaning they showed their true mettle by how they put up with whatever, or whomever, affronted them.

Or it might also signal that life was not meant to be easy. Which, for those paying attention, is a caution about the opening gambit.

Frederick Pottinger was the *ne plus ultra* of one branch of that worthy family. Tall, overbearing and self-assured, he had the misfortune to be the son of a decorated hero, Sir Henry, one whose earlier life had been coloured by romantic adventure, such as the British have long loved. Sir Henry accomplished much on the world stage, meaning (naturally) that of the British Empire; and a grateful country elevated him for it. In due course, the son inherited his wealth, and honours and a title, and squandered it all early, behaving much like a minor character in *Vanity Fair*; however, to give him his due, he mismanaged his inheritance more or less contemporaneously with Thackeray's satire, and so must be allowed his own originality in this. He was sent packing to Australia and reconstituted himself as a mounted policeman, with mixed results and less acclaim than he might have hoped for. Damned colonials.

The book you are doubtfully contemplating at this moment might be regarded as a curious kind of detective fiction. For what follows is about finding evidence and sifting it, identifying and tracking down clues, aligning the traces – all the way to the bitter end. It is not fiction. Everything here is true; or if not, then you are on a promise. You will know when something is just a thought, and in that case what you read will be a deduction rather than an invention. You are in a safe pair of hands here. You can of course check it all for yourselves. Indeed, so you should. No one has invented any of what follows, unless it is the Pottingers themselves.

The narrative ahead of you pursues the course of events across a broad terrain, varied and forbidding and difficult, interpreting as it goes whatever clues are cast about – in order to track down an elusive person of interest, as the authorities might say. And that notion of tracking is appropriate enough, given how it all turns out. In the process you are urged to appreciate the moral stature of our hero, or heroes if you will, for one was the distinguished father of the other and cast his shadow and his fortune where his son was most disposed to benefit. *Noblesse oblige* and all that.

As everyone knows, the skill of a tracker is in identifying where details and items have been ever so slightly disturbed, to observe whenever a line of orientation is suddenly altered, to read at all times the lie of the land. To catch his man, or to catch up with him, if he can. Yet, it is truly amazing what some people can't see, even when it is right in front of them. What one has to do is follow a line, not hunt for every shifted pebble or broken twig. Even if you don't see every tiniest clue, you can work out what is most likely. That is how you do it. Even blind Freddy would have known that.

And just who was blind Freddy? Ah, that's the question.

It has been argued by some that the original blind Freddy was not Sir Frederick Pottinger but a blind hawker in Sydney in the 1920s, famous for finding his way around the city streets and recognising people by their voices.[1] That explanation is not immediately convincing, because written reference to 'blind Freddy' precedes him. And in any case, the expression, as commonly used, is somewhat less than admiring. It remarks instead on the absurdity of someone who fails to see the bleeding obvious.

Another claimant is said to be one Frederick Solomons,[2] who, having turned blind at the age of 11, was a regular at boxing matches in Sydney in the early years of Federation – finding his entertainment in the sound effects perhaps. Again, the circumstance of that character hardly sponsors the inflection we all understand by 'blind Freddy'. And more to the point, even if he were well known in Sydney, that is no reason to suggest why the rest of Australia would have immediately adopted reference to him. For the expression was taken up everywhere, much as was a comparable 'game as Ned Kelly'. The source has to provide some widespread resonance.

Sir Frederick Pottinger is that likeliest source. His reputation was spread all across the country, and the papers, both local and intercolonial, delighted in relating his misadventures. Maybe more scraped than spread, then. Whichever, his name was in front of everyone.

So again we ask: just who was blind Freddy? He may not have known how to answer that himself.

I

THE POTTINGER FOUNDATION

Greatness knows itself.

William Shakespeare, *King Henry IV, Part 1*

FIRST, BECAUSE WE have to start somewhere, a little about the Pottingers.

The Pottingers were something. More to the point, they knew they were something, they always believed that.

They were a family made for greatness. Theirs was a family who had achieved much over a very long time indeed; and they took good care to ensure that the world should know it.

To discover who the Pottingers inherently were, to know their distinction, you have to know about their lineage. That not only goes with the territory, in many respects it *is* the territory. History reveals this as a general principle: that great men and women are the scions of great families. We know them by and through and because of their heritage. Indeed, that is how they know themselves. Notability underwrites nobility.

Or to turn that around another way, the measure of greatness is consequence. That is why Mr John Debrett so helpfully compiled his *Peerage* (1802): to set out the grounds for the pretensions of the great to superiority. Subsequent to that publication – indeed, possibly because it drew such gratifying attention to the benefit of being included in its listing – honours grew more plentiful and further greatness was displayed. Mr John Burke then felt called upon to amass a further such compilation, *A Genealogical and Heraldic Dictionary of the Peerage and Baronetage of the United Kingdom* (1826), more ample and more amplifying. Edifying too, no doubt, if only we would pore over its pages with the proper respect.

But we do not. We neglect the opportunity to fully inform ourselves. Why is the world so mean-spirited about greatness? Especially this end of the world, where we pride ourselves on our genial tolerance of one and all. Demonstrably, that boast has its limits. We say that we welcome anyone – except those who by their conduct seem to suggest they are our betters. Or think they are.

Here in the cartographical afterworld we are impressed by those who fairly win their spurs, but not by those to whom honours are presented on a plate, or a cushion, or however they are served up. We prefer the company of those just like us. Yet isn't it likely that from time to time there will be some whose accomplishments are superior to our own? We should concede that niggling hesitation, for otherwise we expose ourselves to the chancy self-assurance that we are as good as it gets.

The original question is left hovering. Why do we turn against the truly estimable? Why would we not wish to welcome such a one among us, why not acquaint ourselves with greatness in our midst when it reveals itself? After all, there are few enough exemplars of true ingrained greatness readily at hand. Of course not, because by very definition the great are exceptional. Yet, whenever we come across them, we belittle them. We are affronted. Why? Why do we set so little store by them when they grace us with their presence?

Churlishness, damnable churlishness.

Oh, and another thing. Greatness is not to be confused with the merely heroic. All sorts of people perform remarkable deeds, or achieve some remarkable outcome, given an opportunity. That is what an individual may achieve, if brave enough, or adroit enough, or determined. But greatness is innate. You either have it or you don't, and if you have it, then it must be in some important manner inherent, and inherited. And if you don't have it, then tough luck. You missed out.

That is what puts up our hackles. It looks like the lottery has been rigged.

To the Pottingers, then.

Long ago, when that estimable writer Henry Fielding celebrated the greatness of his compatriot Jonathan Wild, he pointed to the customary practice of biographers: that at the beginning of their memoir, those who undertook such a noble enterprise should:

> step a little backwards (as far, indeed, generally as they are able) and trace up their hero, as the ancients did the river Nile, till an incapacity of proceeding higher puts an end to their search.[1]

Now, it might be considered rash to correct so distinguished an authority, but surely Fielding misstated the case here, unless his habitual irony was for once unusually deflected. For such a starting point is not just a matter of custom but, we might say, requisite. The great know the truth of this. That is why they are committed to the continual resurrection and renovation of their own past, to the point of infatuation.

So, to take the plunge into the tepid channel of Fielding's dangerously infested waters: one of the Pottingers was the sovereign of Belfast. Never mind that this was not a true royalty – that is a mere incidental detail. A Thomas Pottinger was named mayor, or 'sovereign', of Belfast when that town was first granted its corporate charter in 1661 – a date to reckon with, coming so soon after the restoration of the English throne. Cromwellian rule, which had proved so oppressive through extensive tracts of Ireland, had been displaced. The Pottingers early and sensibly declared themselves loyalists,[2] and they consolidated a seat for themselves at the very centre of loyalist Ireland. Well, strategically close to one side of it, the British side.

Unfortunately for the family's ambit claim to some sort of esteem by way of a noteworthy ancestry, Belfast had in fact been incorporated nearly 50 years earlier, in 1612, by letters patent from King James; and the first 'sovereign' was one Thomas Vesey. Or John Rigby.[3] It all depends, but in either case an inopportune detail. Not Thomas Pottinger, you see.

Nevertheless, the Pottingers had established themselves in that dewy corner of the world, and well ahead of any troublesome Scottish insurgency. A Pottinger grave in Belfast is dated at 1602. Previous to that doleful marker, an earlier Pottinger had led a troop of mercenaries in the wars of northern Ireland during the reign of Queen Elizabeth (the 'Nine Years' War', 1594–1603), another unhappy time for the Hibernians.[4] It is not suggested of the Pottingers that those two historical traces are directly consequential.

A laneway in Belfast was named for the Pottingers. That is not quite the same as a major thoroughfare; but at least the family was sufficiently important to be commemorated, if less than magnificently. They had made some kind of mark. Or more likely, they had a vested interest – the alleys or 'entries' of Belfast are named for prominent merchants, which 'suggests that they may have well been involved as developers'.[5]

But before indulging ourselves with the succeeding generations of Pottingers and their illustrious attainments, we should persevere in the direction finger-posted by the worthy Henry Fielding.

Were we to paddle further up his steadily diminishing metaphoric waterway, we would discover a real royal connection right at the top of the Pottinger tree – allowing that remarkable botanical specimen to be growing in near proximity to the river bank. Let the record speak for itself. Sir Henry Pottinger, father of the true hero of this present respectful narrative, was by the tally of the College of Heralds thirty-first in line of descent from Egbert, the first Saxon king of England and grandfather of Alfred the Great.[6] There it is, greatness revealed from the very beginning. Could anything be more substantive?

Unhappily though, the ornate rolls of the College of Arms fail to identify Pottinger as a family name in Saxon times.

Even more unhappily, 'there is no confirmation of this royal connection in contemporary Anglo-Saxon manuscripts'.[7] We dismiss that mean-minded reservation as a glitch, a mere lacuna. Nobody complains that Einstein resorted to jump discontinuities in his theorising. Why should we not allow a comparable manoeuvre inside so august an institution as the College of Arms?

At least let us agree on this much: whether or not the trajectory of Fielding's recommended historical trace deviated up a side creek, a slip stream, the Pottingers were most assuredly descended, in 31 (or 32, depending on which of them you have in mind) steps, from someone. How many of us would be so bold as to claim the same?

Any slight misgivings can be dealt with another way, by the revealing and persuasive evidence closer to hand, that Sir Henry's father was named Eldred, an unmistakably and irrefutably Saxon name. Even a significant name, for it means, or might mean, wise counsellor. That is proof demonstrable that the Pottingers knew their roots; or, to continue with Fielding's metaphor, their spring, their source. And it demonstrates how the Pottingers revered their heritage. Not for them any ungenteel contractions like Alf or Fred. Eldred, if you please, and a name that was assigned down, or up, through the generations. In fact, until the sorry and all but conclusive example of Henry's son Frederick, the Pottingers did not think in terms of descent.

That other source of ancestral consequence in Great Britain, the Norman Conquest, is in the case of the Pottingers dubious. More like a billabong alongside Fielding's grand canal.

Muddied. Latter-day editors of *Burke's Peerage*, bedevilled by the responsibility of correcting the imaginative contributions of this vainglorious work's founding father,[8] have protested that too many families claimed an illustrious ancestor who crossed the Channel with William the Conqueror. Think about it. All those claimants with their retinue, and their steeds, and their heavy armour, and their castle-building stonemasons – why, there must have been a very armada to manage it all, and barely enough room left for William himself. All those honourables, columns and columns of them. It gives pause – just which side was drawing the long bow?

Still, we are offered a tempting tidbit of detail. An Alexandre le Potager was favoured by William the Conqueror with a land grant in the wind-riven Orkneys. There is an inaugural endowment for you, a royal keepsake, if somewhat off to one side from the main action. It is not to be sniffed at. A grant is a grant, though some are less prestigious than others.

Provokingly, it has to be confessed that the newfangled latter-day transatlantic Pottingers, the American cousins, enthusiastic in the cause of discovering their true ancestry as only Americans can be, have been cautious about any possible French connection. An explanation is not difficult to find. The name Pottinger derives from Old French 'potager', meaning something like a vegetable patch, a kitchen garden or – more elevated possibly – a maker of stews from those homegrown ingredients. In more recent times, and perhaps not insignificantly, the French *potager* has evolved into a kind of show-off garden, all display and no practical use. So the American Pottingers have chosen instead a Norse connection, recalibrating the family name to 'potting jar', meaning maybe an herbalist or, as in Scotland, an apothecary.[9] Neither of which displays a scintillating origin. None of which suggests the inception of greatness. Scrabbling about with vegetable peelings.

In either case, we can be sure that while the Pottingers were originally of the land, landed certainly, they were not gentry, or not at the beginning. You can see why it might be preferable to attach themselves to Alfred the muffin minder.

The available evidence is not always uniformly reassuring. There does seem to have been someone of the name Pottinger, as distinct from Potager, at about the time of the Conquest. A family of that name settled in Berkshire and from there two branches of Pottingers derive, the elder of them relocating to Ireland. Here they established themselves well enough that by Elizabethan times one was a godson to Sir Walter Raleigh, indeed was named after him, and went with him to Guiana. Not that the venture did him or his family much good, for he died there. He was killed, actually.

The point is that the Pottingers had already begun making connections. The first part of that story hints they were ingratiating themselves rather than demonstrating greatness – and they continued to be, as the saying is, there or thereabout in the unfolding political games to come. In particular, they would ensure that they were in the mix of the Protestant ascendancy.

It is to be noted that Walter was not a name the Pottingers readily gave to their infant boys thereafter.

The unfortunate Walter's younger brother was father of that Thomas Pottinger already noticed, the sovereign of questionable currency. Thomas assisted Arthur Chichester, a figure prominent in King James's strategy of settling Protestants in the north of Ireland and subjugating Ulster in the wake of the lordly chieftains of northern Ireland, who took themselves off to exile. Chichester was appointed Lord Deputy of Ireland in their stead. He was created a baron for his success, not least for establishing a power base at Belfast. Regrettably, Thomas Pottinger was not elevated for his assistance, but he did receive land grants in counties Down and Antrim. King James was imperceptive in this as in other matters of consequence (the blessings of tobacco, for example); he simply failed to appreciate the inherent greatness of the Pottingers.

The family settled in Belfast and turned themselves into successful merchants, with their main place of business thought to be in High Street, close to the Pottinger laneway now known as Pottinger's Entry. Their home was above the business. Greatness so far inhibited. Propriety limited.

Thomas had at least two children, one inevitably and confusingly likewise named Thomas, the other Edward.[10] That older brother, Edward, spent more time at sea than on land. The high-water mark of his career was when, as captain of the *Dartmouth*, he carried William III to Ireland. King William was landed at the mouth of the lough, the great sea inlet, in June 1690 and marched up to Belfast, proceeding from there to his overwhelming victory over James II at the Battle of the Boyne.

The *Dartmouth*, though, had a different, and as it turned out less glorious, mission. Edward set off in the opposite direction, to hunt for and chase down a rumoured French squadron. But like his Great-Uncle Walter, Captain Pottinger derived no benefit from his brief moment of glory, for within days he had lost his ship, his crew, his life and – as the record shows – his name:

> The *Dartmouth* Frigate was ... cast away in the Sound of *Mull*, by falling foul on a Rock, and Captain *Porringer*, with most of the Men, perished in the Water.[11]

Porringer is apt. It returns us to the inaugural kitchen milieu.

In due course the younger brother, the next Thomas Pottinger, acquired the leasehold of property across the river from Belfast, known as Ballymacarrett (McCarrot? Potager?). At that time it was a mostly uninhabited estate, although this might be more properly understood as meaning that the Pottingers were the only residents of note. Their business, said to have involved extensive trade between Belfast and the East Indies, was profitable; though this detail might not be as exactly true as is asserted or not just yet in their evolving history.

We can be confident that they were among the early traders in an expanding field, or whatever is the appropriate maritime equivalent of an acreage. The Pottingers had by now the wherewithal to set about building themselves a substantial and secure residence, a three-storeyed house known as Mountpottinger. A family seat.

Here for the next century the Pottingers sat; from here, to appropriate a line from Stephen Leacock, the younger Pottingers flung themselves upon their steeds, a different kind of mount, and rode madly off in all directions,[12] galloping about the countryside and developing the family passion for horses and horse riding. Henry Pottinger was born there. So too, in 1758, was his father, the aforementioned Eldred (son of yet another Thomas Pottinger, High Sheriff of County Down).

That same Thomas Pottinger, or more likely yet another Thomas Pottinger, undoubtedly closely related, was said to have been the first Presbyterian sovereign of Belfast, in 1689.

Stay with me. There are a few more Thomases to go. In this particular instance, regrettably, we encounter yet another difficulty. For just as with the previous claim to fame, so here the table published in the *Belfast Monthly Magazine* (1810) records no such person, Presbyterian or other, in that role.

But it is a revelation to be informed of that Pottinger affiliation with Presbyterianism. With the rest of Ireland mainly Catholic, and the leading families all Church of Ireland, that is, Anglican, it might be assumed that the Pottingers would have recognised where an advantage lay. As perhaps they did, for the strength of the Scottish influence was in the north, and substantially about Belfast. That was now their most strategic community.

Under James I's programme of 'plantation', Protestant families had been brought to Ireland's northern provinces: some English, increasing numbers of skilled artisans from Belgium and France (the Huguenots), but the majority from lowlands Scotland, together with troublesome reivers, the stubbornly independent border territory people. These were the small-scale farmers who provided the Pottingers and other merchants with their market produce. They were 'planted' on the lands forcibly vacated by the original settlers in the region, mainly Catholic and now (in an ambivalent idiom that would become well understood on the opposite side of the world) dispersed.

The newcomers took over the growing and soaking and spinning of flax from the displaced original tenant farmers, and the weaving of increasingly fine cloth, damask, for example. Flax was left out on the grass to get wet and soften in the heavy dew, or soaked in ponds and dams, in order to release the fibres – retting, it was called, which in some versions of the Belfast dialect might sound close enough to 'rotting'. Then the home-spun unbleached cloth was likewise spread out on the great stretches of green (and doubtless from whence 'lawn'), in the sun and the soft rain. It was this cottage industry that provided the impetus to the linen-making that became Belfast's early claim to fame. Irish linen was prized everywhere, and the best of it came from Belfast.

This was sweet productive farming country too and had carried a very profitable wool industry, although the English appropriated all the Irish wool for themselves, to manufacture their vaunted broadcloth. Export to elsewhere was prohibited, but considerable quantities were smuggled to France and Spain, and the Irish grew wealthy in that way instead, thereby further provoking the sourness of the English. That regulation, effectively prohibiting the Irish from exporting wool and other produce anywhere, was passed in the English Parliament and agreed to by the recently crowned King William. The Irish were encouraged to develop their linen trade in lieu.

They were spectacularly successful. By the end of the eighteenth century, linen accounted for about one-half of Ireland's exports, much of it directed towards the British colonies in North America; it was sent out as both finished furnishing fabric and sailcloth.

A different commercial route was to India and back, returning cargoes of cotton from the factories of the East India Company, and setting up early competition with Liverpool and Manchester. That was an increasingly significant connection. Strong canvas, a blending of linen and cotton, was always in demand for the Company's fleet of ships, while fine Irish table linen suited the taste of the Company officials and their wives, and the rajahs all intent on displaying the acquired elegancy of their living. It awoke the Irish to the potential wealth to be gained from India by respectable trade, as distinct from that other source described as loot – one of the first words the British learned from their presence on the great subcontinent,[13] one of the first words they took back home with them.

The Pottingers shared in the growing wealth of Ulster. On the basis of this wealth the local gentry took to building their grand houses – or renovating long-established ones. Indeed, county Down was home to numerous gentry, some of them impressively grand indeed. Lady Downshire (her not very imaginative patronym says it all) was pre-eminent in the local establishment. Her family seat then was Hillsborough Castle, which years after became the residence of the Governor of Northern Ireland. Viscount Castlereagh was from this county too. They held lands suitable to their status, and houses to match, though Castlereagh's seat was not at first so very great. But his fortune was.

When Eldred Pottinger married Anne Gordon in 1779, he married well. Which is to say that he had accumulated enough wealth to be acceptable as a suitor. The Gordons were a prominent and respectable family, who through an earlier strategic marriage had acquired an estate originally owned – in the time of Charles I – by the Montgomerys; Sir James Montgomery named it Florida House from his love of flowers. That manor house was pulled down and wholly rebuilt of locally quarried grey stone in the years 1780–1800. Alas for those who prefer a touch of romance in their history. No sooner was Anne Gordon out of the original house, than it was demolished, leaving not much more than a date, July 1676, inscribed on a piece of slate and set into a wall in the farmyard.

The course of those who would claim greatness is never easy. The narrative of their lives is littered with all sorts of trials and misadventures, through which they show their mettle. All was not well with the Pottingers, nor with the newly married couple. The family business was not thriving. The evidence? As early as 1750 Mountpottinger had been advertised to let.[14] That was an early sign, a forerunner of a rather more dire change of circumstance later on. In the very year of their marriage, Eldred was obliged to sell his right to Mountpottinger for £18,113 (presumably his share, as his brother and sister would have had an interest, his father and uncle, and likewise his cousins). Three years later, the lands of the estate were sold and then, inevitably, the house itself. The Pottingers were plainly coming down in the world, though their new residence, Craigavad House near Bangor, was certainly handsome.[15]

In addition, at this very time, rather than enjoying his nuptials Eldred Pottinger was busy raising the Mountpottinger Volunteers, a group dedicated to protecting the rights of men like himself, farmers and linen traders. By this action, he identified himself as a radical, or as a patriot, depending on your point of view. Either way, he was distancing himself from the establishment. That was not conducive to maintaining the family's standing, nor did it assist their aspirations.

He had his reasons. It was not all about defending his livelihood. He was an idealist. He espoused the cause of Ireland and the right of the Irish to make decisions for themselves. Like others of his generation, he was excited by the recent and ongoing political agitation in France and America. No doubt it cost him something to marshal and support his assembly of volunteers, for these units all fancied dressy uniforms.

At an early meeting, he presided over a collective decision to pledge themselves to take up arms against the foreign invader, and the affirmation that:

> We do not fear to speak of political liberty for the people of Ireland as voluntary soldiers of this nation. We believe that Ireland should be a nation, independent and free, without impolitic restrictions on our commerce under which we groan.[16]

This was among the first occasions at which the call for Ireland to be regarded and respected as a nation was formalised in public. And with it, the call for political reform. Ireland was becoming restive. So was Eldred Pottinger.

He takes his place in a long line of protest against British – more specifically English – interference in Irish affairs, its enforcing of both social and economic dislocation. There had been many of those, and would continue to be many such, for generations to come. Jonathan Swift's ironic *Drapier's Letters* and his ferocious satire *A Modest Proposal for preventing the Children of poor People in Ireland from being a Burden to their Parents or Country* ..., published at the beginning of the eighteenth century, were among the earliest and most famous of them, although Swift was not necessarily calling for independence. He was more concerned to oblige England to confront its shame.

Ireland's political fortunes had been long entangled. At this stage the momentum of the times was towards the coming Act of Union (1800); with one of the most vexatious concerns being how the populace was to be represented. It was one thing to challenge British interference in local matters, quite another to determine whether the privileged establishment was to continue to hold exclusive political sway, or whether those Catholics disenfranchised by King James's programme of 'plantation' might be included. The Presbyterians, being non-conformist, were not all that much more tolerable. Eldred Pottinger argued for 'full, fair and adequate representation of the people of Ireland in Parliament, without regard to differences of religious opinions'.[17] That meant a parliament that convened in Dublin, not London.

When he subsequently put himself forward as a candidate for election, Eldred Pottinger stood to represent the independent interest, meaning independence from Britain. By and large, he appealed for support from the farmers and merchants in his electorate, the group from which his volunteers had been drawn, the middling range of people from which the

Pottingers had never managed to quite extricate themselves. In these electoral contests, he was unable to meet the expenditure of such a formidably wealthy opponent as Viscount Castlereagh. Castlereagh had a history of investing significant wealth in his campaigns to get himself elected. His election to the seat for county Down in 1790 is said to have been one of the most expensive in Irish history, some £60,000 then.

Pottinger, inescapably a commoner despite his reputed lineage, was not in the same league. When he ran against Castlereagh in 1802, it is needless to say that he attracted comparatively few votes. He could not buy enough of them. The establishment won hands down, but Pottinger's defeat was not for lack of enthusiasm. Eldred had even named one of his sons, born in the midst of all this heady frenetic activity (1792), Charles James Fox Pottinger. This was not as fraught as naming him after Sir Walter Raleigh. Politically, Fox represented all Pottinger's aspirations, but he was personally a less-than-ideal model, notorious as a gambler, a womaniser, and was held responsible for the Prince of Wales's tendency to vomit in public. Indeed, Fox almost predicates the career of Eldred's grandson, Sir Frederick. They both went to Eton, both were given too much money, both went too often to the racecourse, both were licentious. Both were self-indulgent.

It might be presumed that Eldred Pottinger spoke for the common cause, but if so then perhaps not from among the populace. For in an account of events in and around Belfast in October 1796, it is recorded that Eldred Pottinger was one of those landowners whose harvest was cut down by persons unknown, gangs who descended on unsupervised crops and demolished them in an astonishingly short time, sometimes at night, sometimes in the brief interval in which a pipe was being lit: 'Eldred Pottinger Esq. of Mount-pottinger had 12 acres of oats cut down in 13½ minutes ...'[18]

Who, we might wonder, was so meticulously monitoring this frenzied activity, this prodigious work rate? You wouldn't expect regular reapers to work like that. Working like – what is that portentous phrase? – navvies. We might note that none of the great families was caught up in this rampaging sabotage. Certainly not the Stewarts of nearby Mount Stewart. Certainly not Robert Stewart, the taciturn Viscount Castlereagh.

In Pottinger's eyes, Castlereagh was a turncoat. They had shared Whig views in 1790, and they each subscribed to the notion of an independent Ireland. But in 1798 Castlereagh had led the suppression of the Irish rebellion, and the restoration of law and order. That meant he now supported the union with the United Kingdom. So the election in 1802 would be very piquant indeed.

As is all too likely to happen in the political world, deals were done behind doors. Lady Downshire's candidate, Castlereagh's opponent, withdrew his nomination when she was offered an English peerage (with reversion to her son on his majority). Once that had happened, Eldred Pottinger announced that he had no alternative but to abandon his ambitions too, for he had counted on the benefit of her pro-independence influence.

When he was not drilling his volunteers, or campaigning on the hustings, or attempting to forge strategic alliances, Eldred Pottinger was begetting a sizeable progeny. Somewhere it has been remarked that these teeming Irish families coincided with all those potatoes.

His son Henry, the coming man, was the fifth of eight boys, with three sisters intermingled among them. Inevitably, the first of those splendid sons was to be named ... Thomas. That is a characteristic which had not so much run in the family as it had stood permanently clotted in it. But perhaps we might think of it as a commitment to longstanding principle, rather than a collective lack of imagination. This Thomas was, to all intents and purposes, the last of them.

Born in 1783, the eldest of his generation, Thomas the last held a few better cards than the rest of his siblings. Which is not to say he used them wisely. Indeed, playing at cards was not considered the most astute investment in the years leading up to and including the Regency period. Thomas liked to live well. Why not? What else is privilege for?

Henry, his younger brother, was born in 1789, shortly after the fall of the Bastille. Whether that political excitement had anything to do with the birth and naming of Henry's younger brother Charles James Fox belongs to another narrative than this.

The political excitement of these years was rising. Like a true hero in the annals of greatness, Henry's birth is shrouded in mystery. That is another feature he had in common with King Alfred. Some, his kinsman George Pottinger among them,[19] would have it that the auspicious day was Christmas Day. We resist making any indefensible reflections on that remarkable coincidence. Others maintain that his birth was on 3 October. More than this, they are equally insistent that he was born at Mountpottinger, yet as we have already learned Eldred had some years earlier sold his share of the estate. The mystery serves only to excite our interest, as is ever the case when we deal with the incipiently great. When and where exactly was King Alfred born? Can we be certain? The essential likeness, this resurgence of the hallmarks of greatness, becomes uncanny.

The Pottinger boys were given the underpinnings of a good education. Henry attended the famous Belfast Academy, much too young to have joined in another political action, recorded in the pages of the school's early chronicles, of a dangerously radical action undertaken by the older scholars of the day.

For reasons not provided to an enquiring posterity, these boys imagined themselves with a serious grievance, and resolved to take matters into their own hands:

> On the morning of the 12th of April, 1792, eight boarders and two day-scholars shut themselves into the mathematical schoolroom, and declared war against the masters until their requests should be granted. In anticipation of a prolonged siege they had liberally helped themselves to a large quantity of provisions from the kitchen. They had also procured five pistols, and an unlimited supply of powder and shot, and were fully prepared for serious operations. They sent a written dispatch headed 'Liberty Hall' stating fully their demands and refusing to surrender until their requests were granted. Smiths were brought to break open the door. Slaters were sent up on to the roof to pour

> water down the chimney, but all had to retire before the reckless firing of the boys.
>
> At last the Sovereign was sent for to recite the terrors of the law, but the uproar of the battle continued all day, until late at night the unruly boys capitulated. We have no distinct record of the after events ...[20]

There is no sure record that Thomas, the eldest son, was schooled at the Belfast Academy (founded two years after his birth) like his younger brothers; indeed, there is little enough of anything about his early years. He eventually took part in the family's merchant business, married well, and appears to have become somewhat of a playboy. Not necessarily in that order. He was very fond of sailing, and invested both money and time in his sailing boat. Maud Driver, author of a romantic and imaginative history of his son Eldred, the 'hero of Herat', records Thomas's:

> long absences in his yacht; an extravagance that, like many others, had to be foregone when children multiplied and ill-advised speculations failed one after the other ...[21]

When, all too soon, his first wife – and Eldred's mother – died, she left an estate (the unfortunately named Kilbride House, in Kilmore) in trust for their son,[22] the rent from which subsidised his expenses. Thomas was still identified as holding it in trust in 1838,[23] which was an accomplishment of a kind, though he had no freedom to dispose of it. He spent much of his time searching out possibilities for funds (for example, in 1819 he petitioned the Office of the Chief Secretary of Ireland for reparations to moneys he claimed had been lent, rather than gifted, to William III in 1692, some 127 years previously[24]). He attempted to cadge from his own relations too. His children strenuously advised against any ill-advised generosity.[25] Doubtful Thomas.

Such an irresponsible character was duty bound to find his way into the pages of the popular press. In the heyday of the Regency period, the jocular journalists of the time (that may be a tautology; it is certainly too much alliteration) began to allude with a wink and a nod to T. Pot. Teapots. Tommy Teapots. It was simply irresistible, perfectly ridiculous. That is a fair indicator of the reach of Regency wit, a Plimsoll line for it.

Eldred the Elder had problems on his hands, financial problems, and not just those created by his firstborn. He is named in a somewhat pointed aside at the 1803 trial in Downpatrick of Thomas Russell, one of the leaders of the Society of United Irishmen, for high treason. Charged for his part in an attempt at rebellion at the beginning of the year, Russell expressed surprise from the dock at having so little support from several of the jurors who had shared his political views, yet found him guilty. One of those was Eldred Pottinger. That must have been uncomfortable.

He was in no position to provide significantly for his boys. There was one place, however, where a fortune might possibly be made – though they would have to make their own. India. The Pottingers had some knowledge of its possibilities through their trading activities. They knew of the Honourable

East India Company – John Company as it was facetiously known back then – with its 'court' at its head office in Leadenhall Street, London. The boys should be sent out to the Far East forthwith.

Henry had already been extracted from the Belfast Academy and at the age of 12 was sailing as a very young midshipman (1801),[26] apparently unperturbed that his ancestors had no very brilliant record at sea. Even to have signed on as such junior crew would have required connections. So did the very next move. Within a further year he was shipped out to Bombay to try his fortune in the maritime service there.[27] His siblings others would follow to that part of the world in a very little time thereafter.

Not Thomas though. He was to be kept home, under his father's eye. After all, by virtue of primogeniture, the fortunes of the family in that other sense were vested in him. Virtue? As in *virtus in ardua*, the family motto? Hardly. Thomas was more for avoiding difficulties, or extricating himself from them at others' expense.

II

THE NEW DIASPORA

Not all those who wander are lost.

—J.R.R.TOLKIEN, *The Fellowship of the Ring*

IN 1803, HENRY left Belfast for Bombay[1] to find his way in the world. He may have gone on his own or – unlikely but possible – an older brother, Robert, may have accompanied him. Other Pottingers followed in dribs and drabs; even a sister came out later on. There is no ground to suggest she was one of the drabs, but it is possible she was one of the 'fishing fleet': young women, desperate to avoid spinsterdom, going out to India in hopes of marrying into comfortable means. To catch as catch can.

Nearly the whole of Henry's generation of Pottingers relocated to India, most of them to join in the activities of the East India Company; for as Robert Clive ('Clive of India') had notoriously shown, this was the place to seize what opportunity afforded.

Clive's is but one more instance of resourceful greatness. In point of fact the fishing fleet was no different, no less ambitious.

Another of the Pottinger brothers, John, had evidently learned nothing from his family's maritime history either. Chancing his luck, he was briefly a midshipman in the Royal Navy out on the East Indies station, and died at the end of 1807. Two other landlubberly brothers, Robert and Eldred (no, not the heroic one – patently, at this time that had become the next *nom de jour* among the Pottingers), died towards the end of the same year. Here was the family's own skein of 'wild geese':

> The Pottingers, an Irish family, were a prolific source of supply to the Indian Army. In the nineteenth century, at least twelve Pottingers – brothers, cousins, nephews – saw service in the Bombay or Bengal armies; others were in the Indian Civil Service or the British Army. The later generations were mostly educated at Cheltenham. The most famous of the family was Eldred (1811–43), 'the hero of Herat'.[2]

Even at the best of times Bombay was never a healthy place, but especially not when the weather warmed in the middle of the year. The flies were appalling. So was the filth. The sweltering prickly heat was beyond anything that the British had experienced, with numbers of them laid low by heat stroke. Fevers ran rampant in the intense humidity and the heavy rains of the monsoon season. For those who survived, the year's end should have been more tolerable, but even then the nights were sultry.

India was a fatal posting for significant numbers of the British. Apart from fevers and heatstroke, they had to cope with cholera, plague, rabies and smallpox. It took up to five years to build resistance to malaria, typhoid and dysentery; tigers and thuggees were the least of their problems. This was a far cry from the soft green fields of their homeland.

Strings were still being pulled for young Henry Pottinger. He had come to India with the intention of joining the East India Company's marine service (well before the untimely end of his brother John); now moves were being made to alter the terms of his engagement, so that he might be assigned to a cadetship in the East India Company's army. The pickings were much more remunerative in that branch of the service.

The one person who could most effectively arrange that shift was the President of the Board of Control, the official whose role was to mediate between the Governor-General of India (Richard Wellesley – another name to conjure with, another Anglo-Irish connection) and the directors of the East India Company.

That eminent individual, the President of the Board of Control, was none other than the Pottingers' erstwhile county neighbour and local Member of Parliament, Lord Castlereagh. He had sponsored Henry's application in the first instance; now he was asked to transfer that sponsorship to the Company's army.[3] Apart from the awkwardness of requesting a favour upon a favour, it would have required Castlereagh's significant political influence to ensure the alteration, an unusual change. String pulling, without a doubt, and given the extensive bribery and corruption of the previous year's election in Belfast, his part was not impossibly a compensation for Eldred senior's cooperation at the time. Certainly, it is another example of the

Pottingers' ability to contrive and cash in on political favour. In this instance, curry it perhaps.

Either way, this was just one more demonstration of an incontrovertible principle: it is not just who you know that matters, but how you know who you know.

The nub of the matter is that young Henry Pottinger was discovered to have a talent for acquiring the native languages. He was quickly put to work not only in securing a knowledge of these, but to master local idiom. To speak in the native tongue. Tongues. And without sitting on a forbidden cannon like Kipling's young Kim in Lahore, years later. Another Irish.

But there is a downside to speaking in tongues, as will emerge. Pretending to be the thing which is not, in Swift's pointed phrase. Not that that mattered to Kim, nor was Rudyard Kipling particularly perturbed by it.

Henry made good progress in his studies, such good progress that in very short order he was directed, by Major John Malcolm no less, to help with instructing new cadets. Major Malcolm, who had the ear of the Wellesleys, both the Governor-General and the general, was one of the most talented linguists and diplomats in the service of the Honourable Company and had recently returned from his first mission as Envoy to Persia. He was the political advisor to the British army in India, too. It was quite something to have been noticed by Malcolm.

Still in his teens, Henry became an assistant teacher. That might sound more precocious than was actually the case, for English schools at that time commonly called on a senior student to assist in the instruction of the younger children.

This was not quite a comparable circumstance though, for the pupils, all servants of the Honourable Company, would have been rather more select than the scraggy, forlorn and blighted cohort at Dickens's Dotheboys Hall (*Nicholas Nickleby*). More like Belfast Academy. It nevertheless testifies to the young cadet's accomplishment that he had been so readily selected for an advancement, however modest.

That might also sound rather more of a drudge than we would expect of a great man in the making. Yet it holds true to a pattern not unknown in the lives of the great. Think of it as the hero's apprenticeship in some humble station in life. Think of Alfred learning to bake cakes. Those ignoble menial tasks are a caution that the great man must know a lowly status if he is to rise above it. They serve as a reminder of just how far he has to climb, just what obstacles he must overcome right from the outset. What kind of dust he has to leave behind.

Plenty of that in India.

More to the point was young Pottinger's connection with Malcolm at the very outset of his career. That would stand him in good stead. In 1806 he was promoted and made an ensign. Identified as a gentleman too. As though that had ever been in doubt – he knew his worth, he knew his pedigree.

The East India Company's centre of operations on India's western coast was at Bombay – allowing for the centre of anything to be to one side. Not unlike the Pottingers in Belfast, come to think of it. Bombay harbour commanded the Persian Gulf and had defended the Company's interests against the threat of Napoleon, whose incursion into Egypt was not so much to find new design patterns for his dinner service, as – or so he planned, a different order of design – to serve as a base from which to drive the British out of India.

The British authorities were no better informed than the French about the vast territory that lay between Persia and India. Their chief diplomatic activity at this time was to negotiate agreements with the various tribes and potentates of the subcontinent. Their aim was to understand the entangled intersections between all the competing interests, not just in that particular part of the world but over the Himalayas, in the great unknown of that vast and desert interior. Over the hills and far away. They were apprehensive of Persian sallies into Afghanistan, and they noted the actions of the French in negotiating treaties with the Shah of Persia. That did not bode well.

Which is why Major Malcolm had been sent to the royal court in Tehran, to counter the influence of the French in the Middle East. This was the first stirring of what later became known as the 'Great Game', the feints and dodges and subterfuges by which the European powers all tried to second-guess and outwit each other, making reconnoitering forays into the hills and through the mountain defiles and into the deserts, bribing local warlords, entering into secret understandings and tactical treaties, and creating strategic misunderstandings. Above all, avoiding direct confrontation with their rivals. The main activity was concentrated in modern Afghanistan and Pakistan, along the northwest frontier.

The British knew little of this country; their primary effort had been to establish their own authority in and across the subcontinent. They had still to deal with the last vestiges of the Mughal empire, and the Sikhs and the Rajputs; and although they had managed to defeat the confederacy of Marathis in the second Anglo-Maratha war (1803), that would continue to fester until hostilities flared up again a decade or so later. But at this point, their recent victory had opened the way for British agents to begin investigating the valley of the great river Indus, the hinterland of Sindh province. One of them, and one of the earliest, was Henry Pottinger, still a teenager.

He had good reason to shift from the classroom and put his language skills to the test. With that regional war against the Marathi successfully concluded, or apparently so, and with the French driven out of Egypt, the British were now in a strong military and political situation. Young Pottinger was one to seize an opportunity when it came his way. Like his role model Malcolm, he had seen service in those engagements with the Marathi; now he was to survey the new territory and to make recommendations on how to make effective – meaning strategic – use of it.

That much is clear. Not so clear is in what other ways, and how far, he emulated Malcolm. As a young man, Malcolm racked up a number of gambling debts and in all likelihood entertained a *bibi*, a mistress. That, and serious drinking, seemed the sum of a young man's social life in those days. And nights. It was accepted as a perfectly normal arrangement up to and through the early years of colonial India. All the way up the chain of command, the British made such private arrangements for themselves. Even Wellesley, the Governor-General, kept a number of Indian concubines and at the same time became involved with British wives, his excuse, 'I assure you that this climate excites one sexually most terribly'.[4]

It tells a tale that Malcolm was nicknamed 'Boy Malcolm'. Given his customary ebullience, perhaps that adjective was a shortened form of 'boisterous', the only shortening anywhere in his vicinity. He was a huge man, larger than life, massive, well over 6 feet tall. His assistant, Henry Pottinger, an underling, was a mere 5 feet 9 inches, and heavy for his height.[5] Less boisterous too, but a young man nevertheless, and aware of his bachelor status.

Hereabouts (modern-day Pakistan) was not the most prepossessing corner of the subcontinent, although the floodplains about the Indus had been farmed from ancient times, and had for centuries produced vast crops of cotton. But beyond that stretched sandy or rocky desert lands, with water difficult to come by. You had to find your way to the scattering of wells, often at challenging distances from each other.

The Indus valley was a country characterised by occasional palm trees, and otherwise low meagre scrub. It had proved to be the end of the line for Alexander the Great, who was checked in his final battle in India by the vertically challenging king Porus, towering over the much shorter Macedonians not just because he was nearly seven feet tall but because he was sitting atop an elephant, a military transport unknown to the invaders. In the course of the fighting, Alexander's favourite horse Bucephalus was killed, and Alexander himself thrown to the ground. Greek records preserve the aura of the emperor's greatness by recounting that battle as a victory, even though Alexander proceeded no further and withdrew his army, his greatness preserved in the record, but somewhat dented in the event. If Alexander wept, it may not have been because there were no worlds left to conquer, but because he had been stopped.

In 1808, with three of Henry's siblings recently cut down in short order by unspecified illness, young Pottinger undertook a mission to Sindh, to the capital, Hyderabad, escorting an envoy commissioned by the new Governor-General in Calcutta to enter into treaty negotiations. Sindh was of particular concern as it would be the likeliest way the French would approach. Napoleon had read his history and noted Alexander's route. What was good for one great general would undoubtedly prove good enough for another.

The British had yet to deal with the overlords of this territory, the Afghans. Sindh had been divided up among four Baluchi brothers; there were tribal rivalries, religious schisms, and long-persisting feuds – it was all very unstable. But then, that was the case for most of the northern regions.

Sindh was a terrain that had been allowed to degenerate, largely sterile except along the course of the Indus river, dusty and dry, with desert waste in one direction and massive rocky mountains hemming it in on another, and the sea in yet another. Good for scorpions but not much else. The British interest in it was political rather than economic. And strategic: they had in mind to use the river for access to the northwest frontier.

But the Indus was difficult. The exhausted Indus valley itself ended not unlike the Nile in a vast meandering and malarial delta – the opposite and unhelpful end of Fielding's pattern for the histories of the great. That delta was and still is largely a tangle of reeds and channels. Mangroves have marched out to sea and along the coast, misleading rivulets curl and widen and narrow and abruptly end, and all too often the sea surges in and overruns all.

Henry Fielding was, as may be remembered, especially interested in the ultimate source of the lives of the great. But then we must also think about what his portentous image tells us about their likely issue. For, unfortunately, the downstream end of these major watercourses fritters away in those desultory deltas; and that is unhappily all too pertinent in the case of the Pottingers. They followed an irresistible surge towards greatness, but like the grand rivers their course turned to the very type of ultimate dissolution. A self-dispersal. Futile, really.

The Indus had debouched into the Rann of Kutch. (That is exactly the sort of placename that so delighted Edward Lear – the Hindu Kush, the Akond of Swat, Tonk ... all names to conjure with. Likewise, Lear celebrated his glee in a poetic tribute to, and warning of, the strictures of 'The Cummerbund'.) A decade later though, in 1819, the great river was permanently diverted by an earthquake. So this proved to be unstable geography, as well as unsatisfactory history, which did not augur well for how and where the Pottingers would wash up. It is a testament to Henry Fielding's deep respect for the great that he remained silent about any inconvenient reflections river deltas might throw upon a family line.

Between the ancient town of Thatta (Alexander's point of withdrawal from the subcontinent, though history puts an improved gloss on that and records the great general was setting out for Babylon) and Hyderabad, the wealthy capital of

India's largest princely state, the Indus usually had more than enough depth of water for river traffic. Nonetheless it was advisable to follow the main channels if you could.

The purpose of the new delegation was to undo some of the damage written into a treaty negotiated by the Mumbai Resident and to convey more politically astute requirements by the Calcutta Presidency. This was just the kind of work to whet Henry Pottinger's interest. But the unspoken purpose was to determine where the main channels of the Indus lay.

One-half of the British delegation travelled by local flat-bottomed boat upstream to the seat of government, the other overlanded. These were in fact two ways to surreptitiously survey the lie of the land. The various tribesmen had been right. They mistrusted any activity undertaken by the British, the *feringhee*. Indeed, these last remnants of the Mughal empire were even more suspicious than the Hindi, though neither population appreciated the grasping intrusiveness of the British.

On this diplomatic mission to Sindh, Pottinger was appointed to serve as both an escort and – unofficially – as a 'surveyor'. That is to say, he was to take in whatever information he could about the lands, their productivity, local defences, river crossings, water and fuel resources, and report on it all. He was, in other words, a spy – just as the locals suspected. He fooled nobody. For the British, there just had to be considerable commercial advantage in so much water coming down the river, and they could not be persuaded otherwise. Henry was to pay attention to prospective channels. The Honourable Company had in mind sending up their shipping, moving both cargo and armaments.

Undoubtedly, Pottinger was appointed because of his language skills, though his role as third assistant shows his foot on the lowest rung of a political rather than military career. His linguistic and cultural awareness was very quickly brought into play, as was that of his immediate superior, a Captain Charles Christie. They were embroiled almost at once in complications about expected forms of address and ceremonial greeting, an evasive complaint used by the Sindhi functionaries as grounds for stalling the delegation's progress.

Henry did not accept this kind of dissimulation at all well. It encouraged early in his career what would become an ingrained disdain, if not contempt, for the customs and practice of local peoples, regardless of their status. Pottinger's attitude was that the local population should recognise their superiors and acknowledge the authority of the British flag (either the Union Jack, or the somewhat American-looking flag of the East India Company). He mistrusted the natives one and all; he had already the admirable heroic virtue of contempt for meanness, mendacity, evasiveness, ignorance. In a word, inferiority.

Even at this rudimentary stage of his career, he was developing his own trenchant style. Exasperated by the blatant stone-walling of the Sindhians when the British sought to begin their expedition to Hyderabad, he harrumphed at their attempt at 'imposing punctilious ceremonies upon foreigners',[6] and denounced it. This kind of proceeding 'should be crushed', for otherwise, in future, British envoys would find themselves 'cramped by litigious etiquette'. He was exasperated by their disingenuousness, though it did not occur to him that they, the British, were just as equivocal. Which, of course, is exactly the way diplomacy works.

He reported on the course of the great river, its branches and tributaries, its depths and its flow, its increasing breadth – sometimes miles wide – and at occasional convergences its astonishing turbulence. Like the Ganges, it flowed through alluvial plains, which meant that the banks were unstable and might be undercut, so increasing the quantity of silt carried downstream and deposited there. Like the Nile, it flooded regularly, leaving such ancient towns as Thatta awash for months at a time, the countryside all a sea of mud. Jungle beyond that. Sometimes Pottinger detected small waterways branching off but proceeding nowhere, another aberrant complication for those intent on identifying the Indus as a pattern of greatness.

Pottinger found little to recommend this part of the world to the attention of his superiors. The people – the Sindhians – 'are avaricious, full of deceit, cruel, ungrateful, and strangers to veracity'.[7] They were every bit as obnoxious as those self-important officials whom he was subsequently to encounter in Balochistan. There was a saving grace, however, and a telling one. The women were extraordinarily beautiful. Lighter complexioned, though he did not say so:

> The beauty of their women is proverbial, and deservedly so ... among the numerous sets of dancing girls, who came at different times to exhibit before us, I do not remember to have seen one who was not distinguished by loveliness of face, or the symmetry of her figure, and in most

> instances, both these requisites to beauty were strikingly combined.[8]

These were *nautch* girls, selected for their beauty, and Pottinger was duly appreciative; though his anxiety about their symmetry seems whimsical. They were not the kind of women who went to the wells carrying great metal pots on their head for water. They were themselves ornaments to the sumptuous courts of the amirs, the rulers of the smaller states. Pottinger was quite interested in what at the time was coyly acknowledged as female charm. He was a young man, after all; and this was, as the Governor-General himself had noted, a warm climate.

III

JUST DESERTS

The voice of one crying in the wilderness.

—BOOK OF ISAIAH

ON THE SATISFACTORY completion of this diplomatic mission, fate intervened once more, as so often it does in assisting the great. General Malcolm (he had been promoted) was to have established an embassy at the court of the Shah of Persia, but the political landscape changed and his invitation was cancelled. He had intended to use his travelling there as a pretext for surveying the country between India and Tehran and assessing the likeliest route an attacking army might take, the French, for example, or maybe Russian, allied to an increasingly frisky Persia. Unable to carry out this surveillance personally, he was pleased when his two young protégés volunteered to undertake the daring mission themselves, deep into unfamiliar territory, to explore the unknown lands to the north, beyond the Hindu Kush.

At the beginning of the year 1810, in the deep midwinter, newly promoted Lieutenant Pottinger, together with his immediate superior on the Sindh mission, Captain Charles

Christie – scion of the famous London auction house[1] – set out from Bombay in a small sailing craft, bobbing out to sea and up towards the Persian Gulf, bypassing the restless eyes of Karachi. Their plan was to avoid scrutiny as far as possible, for they were well aware of the deep-seated suspicion and resentment of the local population. And they had a clever stratagem. They would disguise themselves as Muslim horse dealers, supposedly in the employ of a well-known agent, and with several genuine horse dealers, Afghans, accompanying them. Also, a couple of Hindustani servants. What could go wrong?

Besides, Henry Pottinger for one knew a good deal about horses. We may imagine his attachment from an early age, when he first straddled a rocking horse in the nursery without ever looking as if he might fall off. Once seated, he was not going to yield to his brothers. Given his subsequent career, that is a reasonable deduction. Yet, despite those early signs of innate skill and tenacity, in Bombay he had enlisted with the infantry, not the cavalry. Truly, the ways of the great are a mystery to the rest of us. Unless, of course, the expense of it was beyond him at that stage. He would have had his reasons.

Several days later, in the evening, Pottinger and Christie landed at a small harbour a good distance further up the coast, and set about improving their disguise, rubbing a stain into their skin: 'we completely metamorphosed ourselves, by having our heads shaved and adopting the entire native costume'.[2] This anchorage, Sonmiani, on the edge of an unprepossessing and mainly arid if not scalded landscape, was another location with rich historic overtones, for Alexander's navy had sheltered here while awaiting their rendezvous with his army.

Pottinger was careful to spell out the connection. Perhaps he had intimations of another historical passage; at the very least he recognised his own intersection with the grand narrative of the past.

This was an ideal starting point for their expedition into and through the wilds of Balochistan. They would traverse sparsely covered country, sparsely watered as well, and unpopulated; elsewhere, regions of jungle. In either case, uncultivated – or, as the British tended to envisage such terrain, uncivilised. The colonisers held the same view of Australia.

That was the plan, to avoid encountering anything or anybody as far as possible, until they were well away from the coast. Puzzlingly, they chose to travel by camel, even though they were meant to be horse dealers. It was their choice, a practical choice, given deserts and an erratic water supply, if somewhat inconsistent with their disguise and their experience.

It was an extraordinary feint, if that is what it was. By common report, horses and camels don't mix. Blind Freddy could have told them that. What was the point of that manoeuvre? We can only suppose that the secret agents intended to thoroughly confuse those on whom they were spying.

For all the fearsome reputation of the Balochis, Pottinger found them 'extremely indolent', given to smoking and gambling and chewing opium and bhang.[3] It would be a brave man, however, or an obtuse one, who underestimated their resolve to defend their poppy fields, or who mocked their long-barrelled rifles, renowned for their accuracy over an extended range. Down on to narrow winding paths along mountain passes, for example.

The two British and their little party of attendants and fellow travellers crossed the extensive barren plains, with dry-looking trees – if any – withered grass, and, often enough, rocky hills bulging out of the nearby landscape. Their chief concern, to avoid encountering others as much as possible, was well advised.

Eventually, heading always further and further north, the sham horse dealers came to Khelat, a town of mud brick houses and stony laneways, but with a strange rock elevation at its centre, and a fortified structure on its top: the khan's palace, of sorts, the only building that looked capable of significant military resistance.

Pottinger and Christie had kept up a disarming confidence in their disguise as equine traders, especially as their beards grew; and in their powers of deception. Justified, apparently, because they had not been shot. Whether that is different from being shot *at* is not recorded. But then an Afghan visitor to the house in which they were staying declared to those present that he had seen them in Sindh the year before. It disconcerted them to be so readily recognised, and they of course denied it. Matters were smoothed over by others present at the time, who proposed that the two strangers would be embarrassed by having come down in life from officers to traders, and politeness demanded that their hosts discuss other matters. The question of whether they had been officers was left hanging dangerously in the air. All that was missing was a gallows.

The two young men resorted to other stratagems. When their luggage arrived, they opened their medicine chest and set about dosing those who clamoured for aid, supplying purgatives and tonics and pills, remedies for beauty and fertility (just what British officers travelling in disguise might take with them), and hoped for an auspicious outcome. They paid particular attention to the defensive strengths of the town, and its resources. That was the point of their survey, after all. But their past was also catching up with them, in the form of messages from further down the line advising the khan (in Kandahar for the cold season) of what they were up to, that they were secret agents and their business was to assess prospective routes into the territory. Reports also arrived that the amirs in Hyderabad were sending men to bring back the *feringhee*. The longer these two stayed, no longer incognito, the more precarious their circumstance became.

It was now both cold and wet. Indeed, when they had first arrived at Khelat, their whole party was shivering; and as a helpful gesture, they had been made a present of a bag of snow:

> It was the first I had seen, except at a distance on our route up, for nearly seven years, and brought my native green isle, if possible, more forcibly to my remembrance, with all its tender ties and dearest hopes: the feelings attach an inseparable idea of home to any thing, however unimportant, which we have been accustomed to behold in our more juvenile days … I contemplated the snow with a mixed sensation of satisfaction and regret.[4]

Pottinger, his true greatness emerging, was not given to such unworthy reflections as nostalgia, and he was unaccustomed to sentiment. Here though we find him ploughing through drifts of words and displaying an unexpected pomposity in his moral reflections. The ungainliness of his writing is further proof, if we needed it, that he was born to transcend such pettiness. At the time of this episode he was still only 20, though he did not write it up for another four years.

Because he was a young man still, a red-blooded, red-coated (when in his dress uniform) British soldier, he allowed himself an ongoing natural curiosity about the charms of the opposite sex. He could not fail to notice, and remark on, the dress of the Balochi. Even in such near-freezing conditions as they were all experiencing, the men wore a calico shirt open about 14 inches down the front, and the women's attire was very similar, their shifts 'open in front below the bosom, and as they wear nothing under them, their persons are considerably exposed'.[5] He does not appear to have been overly concerned whether they were warm enough. Nor was he worried about symmetry here.

The two travellers left Khelat hurriedly, and by a ruse, along a rugged track that twisted up the steep slopes, until it was no more than a precarious path cut along ledges part-way up the forbidding dark cliffs. At times it was less than two feet wide and they looked down on a dizzying abyss, a quarter of a mile deep. Discretion prevailed over valour and they took to leading their animals along the narrow defile. In miserably cold conditions they slowly wended their way up and up, the country bleak and barren, water in short supply even though far below them it rushed abundantly.

They were an easy target if that had been the intention. Their costume, their guides, and their small travelling party must have worked the trick. Paradoxically, they were delighted with the difficulties which beset them. This was no route for an invading army, and should either the French or the Russians or indeed the Persians attempt it, the ravine was easily defensible. All that was required were a few strategically placed cannon.

And then, like stout Cortes on Darien, they stepped suddenly into another world. 'The desert burst on our view, extending as far as the eye could trace, with the semblance of a smooth ocean from the reflection of the sun on the sand.'[6] Given the family record of the Pottingers at sea, Henry might have chosen a more judicious simile.

They had attained their object, though not yet their next destination, Nushki in the north of Balochistan, well beyond the reach of Edward Lear's sense of nominal absurdity. First they had to manage a long descent, following along riverbeds. These occasionally ran with a little water, but mainly their course was a rubble of worn stone. From there the travellers emerged to the desert plains, watching out for rare oases, and finding their way to the desiccated little town without undue anxiety, leaving the great chain of mountains behind them.

At Nushki they were reminded of the difficulties that surrounded them, made aware of just how dangerous it would be to travel through the desert lands ahead, and not merely because of the dire conditions. They were advised they were certain to be plundered, including of the clothes they stood in; they might well be murdered. And they were challenged to identify what kind of Muslim they were. As it happened, they were both able to recite the Sunni creed, and they discovered the public advantage of a beard, for stroking in the manner of the prophet.

It is a tribute to the efficacy of the East India Company's training that they had such skills to hand; though whether the Honourable Company had been altogether so honourable in this sham is a moot point.

The best of British sterling, they resolved to go on. They had no passport, no letters of introduction, no safety. They had their commission, however, a duty to fulfil. They reduced their baggage to the barest pittance – they would show themselves as too poor to be worth robbing. They would make themselves a small target, like a politician in an election. And to attract less attention they agreed to split up, with Christie going on to Khelat in Afghanistan and Pottinger to Kerman, still in Balochistan but now in modern-day Iran. Although this arrangement was at odds with their orders, they would be able to double the reach of their investigation.

Christie set off in the midst of foul weather, just after a sandstorm, with cloud and thunderclaps foretelling a deluge of rain. He anticipated that Pottinger would arrive at Kerman on the other side of the desert in 40 days and 40 nights. By great good fortune they were not too close to Mt Ararat. Pottinger, his shelter not in the least rainproof, was left sitting in mud. He waited there until the weather improved, following his own path some days later.

Heading out into the desert opened the way for Pottinger to confront his destiny – an odd turn of phrase, as though there might be some other alternative. How would you avoid it? He and his party of five trailed slowly over sandy country, passing historical relics and ancient tombs, deserted villages and deep wells, with water beyond reach, if at all. Sand dunes kept them company on the plains, but at times their path became stony as they wound around the foothills of lofty mountain ranges, through rocky valleys and along dry riverbeds. For three days he wrestled with a fever – the very devil of a fever no doubt. The harsh conditions had all but destroyed pitiful attempts by villagers to sow a crop; and whatever little success they had managed was liable to defeat by hordes of locusts, an apt emblem of drought and famine.

The going got harder as the sand became softer. Soon the little party was caught up amongst waves of sand dunes, steep on the downwind face, and up which they had to clamber, leading their tired and famished camels and urging them on. There was no vegetation whatsoever in this country, and not because of locusts.

Gradually the fine desert sand congealed into hard black gravel. This was a different kind of torment; so too the scorching wind, the simoom, capable of killing man and beast by the ferocity of its heat. Thirst, hunger, fatigue, all were compounded by uncertainty about their way.

They came to a village with a dangerous reputation. A messenger had ridden ahead to ensure that they would be welcome, returning with the answer that as they were now beyond the khan's domain their security rested on Pottinger presenting himself as a Muslim, even better as a pilgrim, and better again as a holy man. Anything for a safe pass.

This might be considered by some to be the very height of foolhardiness. Pottinger would be putting himself in extreme danger if his disguise were penetrated; the worst of infidels. He would have to be confident of his mastery of points of theology, as well as of custom. If he faltered in the least, he would be exposed. Yet here is a fine example of how and why the great are great, and the rest of us are not. It was a masterly decision, brilliant in its audacity. It was so daring as to become a wonderful cover. It was exactly the opposite of what anyone who was suspicious of him would expect him to do. And he knew he had passed muster at least once before, when he recited the Sunni creed.

But it positions him in a new light. He was to be a holy man, spending 40 days in the wilderness. That is fraught with biblical suggestion. He was to be tested in his resolve. He had to find an inner strength.

And that gives us cause to reconsider his birthday. Because significant events like that don't happen to just anybody.

At the very least, his deception would appear problematic. Yet, once more we discern the inherent greatness of the man. He had a mission to complete, a mission for his country. Besides, his conscience was clear if he were not offending against his own beliefs. He could dismiss any hesitation in that regard; indeed, he rather enjoyed demonstrating his prowess in not only avoiding controversy but in settling points of theological debate – as was only fitting for a holy man. He attended prayers at a mosque, 'simply [going] through the motions of prostration'.[7] He conceded no sacrilege in that, even though his fellow worshippers might well have taken offence. At another village, invited by a mullah to a humble meal, he was asked to offer a prayer of thanks, and resorted to stroking his beard and mumbling a few common phrases. These were recounted as examples of how he had maintained his cover, and his own self-respect too, apparently; and indirectly – and indiscreetly – reveals his private estimation of Muslim forms of devotion.

The glare from his extended travels over the vast plains began to affect his eyesight. They – his eyes – became inflamed, and he took to tying a black handkerchief over his turban to cover his face. That limited his observations for the next while though it does not appear there was much of interest on which to comment. As his little band ventured further into the expanse of desert in front of them, he encountered a mirage floating all about, mocking their thirst and possibly calling into question just what could be seen through his black handkerchief. He was likewise bemused by traipsing through over-heated country yet with the sight of snow on the distant mountain tops. Again, through a veil.

From about this time too, his strength of character, his determination to attain his goal, began to show itself. To a lesser person it might show as impatience. The great are moved by higher ambitions. When a village chief became too officious, Pottinger threw aside his pretence and, proclaiming himself an Englishman, dressed down the 'impudent scoundrel' in fine style. In another town he was challenged about Christian belief 'at which I had the greatest difficulty in restraining my temper'[8] but in front of a large crowd managed to rout a sneering cleric by turning his question – where was the Almighty? – against him: Pottinger's response, admired by the assembled townspeople, was to ask where the Almighty was not present.

Was that not a fair imitation of a holy man, one who had derived insight from his time in the desert? Behind a darkened veil, too. Equally, of one who had taken assurance in his own cultural convictions. He was well on the way to becoming what he would be.

After three months of arduous travel through the dry and dusty lands of Balochistan and into Persia, Pottinger finally reached Kerman, where he had arranged to meet up with Captain Christie. He had taken more than twice the estimated time to reach his destination. But Christie had not arrived there either. So Pottinger went on towards Shiraz.

The country continued bare and parched, with ragged barren ranges, useless ravines, and an endless haze of dust, which made for soft evening colours but which were falsely encouraging, just like the mirages; and as alluring as the snow on the top of the distant mountains. All about was either sifting sand or fractured stone, almost a rubble. Increasingly though, in the larger towns he began to see examples of formal gardens and the benefit of accessible water. Indeed, the country became more and more fertile as he approached Shiraz, with the fragrance of roses currently in bloom, and fields of tobacco, 'the mildest and best in the world'.[9] This was more like the Pottinger ideal, a far cry from any ancestral vegetable patch. But from his remarks we deduce somewhat of his experience in the officers' mess back in Bombay. He made no such claims for the tobacco he had smoked through hookahs and the like ('qalyans') on his travels.

He admired much of the local manufacture, especially the exquisitely beautiful flowered silks; he had likewise been impressed with elegant shawls in the earlier stages in his journey. These were not what a quondam holy man should have interested himself in, nor a commissioned officer reporting on the military strengths and weaknesses of this unknown terrain. It is a surprise to see this aesthetic side to Pottinger's character, though he had already shown his appreciation of some forms of beauty. No, these were gifts for someone. Yet, unless his sister had arrived by this time, he had no kinswoman in India.

He did not warm to the Persians themselves, however – he thought them vain, avaricious, sordid and dishonest. He reported them as debauched. He had observed them closely.

Pottinger's tastes were for sterner matters. He took the opportunity to visit Persepolis, a little distance from Shiraz, to view the famed ruins. In this he had all but completed a circuit, because the destruction there had been wrought by Alexander. At long last, at Isfahan, where the main roads to Tehran and Baghdad divide, he met again with Captain Christie. They did not at first recognise each other, for it was evening and Christie's features were not easily identified. Christie, for his part, could not see past Pottinger's Persian costume; and they were both so weatherbeaten as to look more like the local populace than Europeans, *feringhee*.

Pottinger's had been an heroic exploit. He had travelled something like 2500 miles through unknown and uncharted country, much of it on his own – discounting guides, cameleers, servants, messengers and matchlockmen (guards). This was country of which, as the various press notices remarked, nothing had been known since Alexander the Great passed through on his return from India. Lieutenant Pottinger had put his life at risk over an extended period, by posing as a Muslim and indeed as a holy man among a community of fervent believers. He had shown coolness in difficult situations, excepting whenever he lost his temper. He had revealed his innate greatness in setting aside his principles when necessary to turn back against his foes the very treachery he so despised in them, knowing he must be treacherous himself in living a life of guile among them. And he had returned with masses of information of just the kind that the British military sought.

> All this he accomplished with adroit aplomb. What he was less good at was reacting sensitively to local chiefs, headmen, clerics, sentries and court henchmen; he frequently made enemies of them and thus complicated his own progress. This trait of his personality was to endure and, as he rose through the ranks of the army to become a senior administrator, it was to become a handicap.[10]

He was a British bulldog in the making.

With his mission accomplished, he was free to return down the gulf, taking passage on the *Psyche*, from the port of Basrah, along with his silks and shawls and tobacco and leaving the immense, sun-blasted reaches of Balochistan behind him, the thistles and locusts and opium poppies. He reached Bombay in the deep mid-winter, February 1811.

IV

THE SPYMASTER

Oh, what a tangled web we weave …

—SIR WALTER SCOTT, *Marmion*

IT WOULD SEEM to have been unfortunate timing. On his return to Bombay, Pottinger of course reported to his superiors; but his mentor, Malcolm, was at Mysore, preparing to return to Britain on five years furlough, and to receive his knighthood. We can deduce that Malcolm had looked out for his protégé, however, for Pottinger was assigned by the Governor to assist the next rising star in the East, Mountstuart Elphinstone, recently appointed to be the British Resident at Poona.

Maharashtra, in India's northwest, seemed at first to be a tractable territory; but as Pottinger had complained earlier, appearances could be deceptive. The various chiefs were hostile to the British, dangerously so. Their recent defeat had not given rise to spontaneous feelings of gratitude and loyalty. Perhaps that was unsurprising, as they had not had sufficient time to appreciate the benefits of cooperating with the East India Company, and of assigning their taxes to the rigorous supervision of the *feringhee*.

For the time being, both Elphinstone and Pottinger applied themselves to writing books, utilising the resources of the young Bombay Asiatic Society in its grand Parthenon-style building, where the Bombay Geographical Society, the Geological Society and the Literary Society of Bombay all shared the facilities. Elphinstone presented a manuscript copy of Dante's *Divine Comedy*: we ought not innocently presume that it was in Dante's hand, but you never know. Elphinstone's own book, based on his tour of duty as the first British Envoy to Kabul, was published in 1815; Pottinger's account of his travels in Balochistan came out the year following. It would have been bad form to pip his superior at the post.

In these years young Pottinger busied himself acquiring masses of information about the ancient history of the Middle East, in order to establish the basis of his writing as authoritative. But he was also alert to recent discoveries of Greek coinage in the remote and ruined desert country, evidence of Alexander's route. These, and various inscriptions, were a kind of cultural mapping. Pottinger felt the thrill of it.

He had at the same time to attend to his official work. That meant riding about his allocated territory, keeping an eye on matters, delivering important documents, carrying key despatches, and attending the court of the Peshwa (in effect, the Prime Minister of the Maratha Empire). He was not just some insignificant subordinate in the comings and goings of the East India Company. He was privy to sensitive material, and to the formation of policy. From time to time, whenever

Elphinstone was absent, he acted as Resident. If he did not have a price on his head, he would be quite a useful hostage for any of the lawless bands that roamed the countryside, and for those hostile chiefs whose resistance to the British was barely concealed. Pottinger needed to take care.

In 1817, at a time of high tension, just before the third Maratha war broke out, Pottinger – now promoted to Captain – was travelling back from brief leave in Bombay to Poona, leading three horses. That might suggest he had not altogether relinquished attachment to his previous 'character', or that he was keeping his hand in. At the travellers' bungalow outside a village somewhere along his way, on the red soil plains between Bombay and Poona, he observed several Maratha horsemen passing and then repassing in front of the lodge. Knowing the general feeling of the times, he suspected their interest was not impartial; they were patrolling the countryside with intent, and a British officer had recently been speared in that neighbourhood.

He called for his own horse, his trusty mount, renowned throughout the vast Deccan plateau and rejoicing in the name of Bandicoot. That is in fact the name of an Indian rat, a large rat, and hardly the sobriquet for a hero's steed. Not quite the equal of Alexander's ox-headed Bucephalus, for example, even if as we might suspect Pottinger's horse had a long nose. Either that, or it was uncommonly large. The horse too.

Yet here is another of those disturbing significations that hallmark the escutcheons of the great. In choosing to name his horse thus, Henry Pottinger was prefiguring something of his son's history – even though he had yet to marry; he had no progeny. Certainly, he could not have foretold that a conjectural son would make a name for himself in Australia, home of the strange long-nosed and notoriously miserable marsupial of that same name.

More astonishing still, this curious little feral fossicker has given rise to an Australian idiom, 'blind as a bandicoot'. That is such a remarkable coincidence as to be in some sense preordained. It seems to affirm a kind of familial prefiguring; for surely this chain of association augurs fearless Freddy, Henry's son. Truly, the lives of the great trace out paths utterly unlike those of the rest of us.

Waiting until the horsemen had headed a little way up the road on one of their restless criss-crossings, Henry mounted and galloped off across country familiar to him, having hunted there from time to time. He was immediately pursued, sometimes quite closely, but Bandicoot, a young horse of the famous Arabian breed, outstripped them; and so he made his way safely back to Poona.[1]

Which should have been quite enough excitement for the time being; yet the very next day he was involved in the battle of Kirki, the beginning of the third Anglo-Maratha wars, in which he fought with sufficient distinction to be mentioned in despatches.

Greatness everywhere, scattered about like the litter left behind at a racing carnival.

At the age of 30, Henry Pottinger was on the way to consolidating into a more substantial figure. He had become Elphinstone's reliable right-hand man; and he was about to be elevated to a yet more responsible role. After the defeat of the Marathi, he was appointed Collector at Ahmednagar. That meant he not only oversaw the collection of taxes (one considerable source of the Company's considerable wealth) but superintended the police, and sat as chief magistrate for important cases in his district, both of local disputes and criminal matters.[2] To the uninquisitive eye, that merely suggests he had grown in prestige in the Company's service. To those whose discernment has been based on such telling character sketches as in Thackeray's *Vanity Fair*, we would expect to find this becoming the basis for accumulating a modicum of wealth, as well as a little weight. Jos Sedley, the Collector of Boggley Wallah – Thackeray did not have Edward Lear's genius for discovering improbable Indian place names – is a very travesty of Pottinger, in everything except that sure foundation.

Not that Pottinger had become fabulously rich, or not just yet. But it tells us how he was being rewarded for his previous efforts. And it confirms the likelihood of a detail hinted at in a note to the previous page. What, dear reader, you neglected to pick that up? But why do you think endnotes are provided? That is where the choicest morsels from the narrative fare are to be found. There, at the back of the main plot, as any bandicoot could tell you. A vegetable plot. A potager.

His was a role that demanded impeccable behaviour. Time, then, for Henry Pottinger to become respectable. He had been mentioned in despatches, he had won promotion, he had published a well-received book, he had been elected to membership of respectable societies, he was the confidant of a resident and he circulated around the edges of the Governor's circle. What he needed was a respectable wife.

He found one. On 9 September 1820, so the press reported, Captain Henry Pottinger, Collector at Ahmednuggar (Ahmednagar), was married by a Company chaplain, Rev. Thomas Carr, to Susanna Maria Cooke, in St Thomas's Church, Bombay.[3] It was appropriate for him to marry, and appropriate too to choose so prestigious a venue, for this was the very church the Governor attended. Elphinstone though was not committed to formal worship. Nor was Elphinstone committed to formal relationships. He never married, but:

> carried on sexual liaisons with British and Indian women with the relish of a true Georgian, ranging from prostitutes to well-born ladies. Unsurprisingly, he occasionally contracted venereal diseases, which he treated with ointments of sulphur and mercury.[4]

Nevertheless, he evidently approved when, as was the custom of the time, Pottinger asked his superior's permission.[5] Elphinstone was not given to irony.

Miss Cooke was the daughter of the late Captain Richard Cooke, originally of Cookesborough, county Westmeath,[6] but afterwards Dublin, where she was born. Her father's recent decease suggests she may now have been on the market. She needed to find a husband as Pottinger needed to find a wife; and where better to go trawling than out in India? Doubtless she was one of the fishing fleet too, and the interested parties could not afford to shilly-shally, because while the competition among the eligible young men was fierce, single young women needed to cement their connection promptly, for reputation's sake. Though we can safely guess there were more than one or two Becky Sharpe adventuresses among their number.

It is most unlikely that Henry Pottinger had known or known of Susanna in Ireland. He left there at the age of 14, when she was only three; that would have been a precocious attraction. Besides, the two families lived a hundred miles from each other. Nor did Pottinger take leave to return to Ireland in quest of a suitable match. He stayed on his own patch. Cooke had been in the army and in all likelihood went to the Peninsular wars; Pottinger was a Company man. Pottinger had to have encountered her somewhere, but he had not left India, he had not left the Deccan other than for his famous adventure into the Persian deserts. She had to have found her own way to fashionable Bombay, fashionable for the fishing fleet to find anchorage.

Pottinger would have been attracted by her beauty – even years later, in her middle age, she was acknowledged as such.[7] If she carried a small fortune with her, Pottinger would have found that agreeable too. For her part, he was on the rungs of a secure career, he had prospects, and he could now afford a wife. (He already had a horse, and he had that cache of pashmina shawls and embroidered silks, unless those had already been distributed to other ladies of his acquaintance.) This was precisely the sort of marriage to be hoped for.[8]

What she would not have been expecting was to be carried off further into the desolate lands of the interior, to unprepossessing, drought-beset Ahmednagar.[9] There would have been very little of whatever social whirl she briefly enjoyed in Bombay; the wedding was just after the monsoons had finished, and the dry weather was returning. That would have been testing for her, fresh out from Ireland. That corner of the subcontinent was – is – notorious for its astonishing floods and devastating droughts.

With an overplus of Wellesley's warm weather, the new couple promptly set about raising a family. Their first-born, son and heir to the line, came into that trying part of the world in October of the following year, after the monsoons. It would become hot again quite soon enough.

He was named Eldred Elphinstone, honouring both his grandfather and the family's Saxon patrimony, and also his godfather the Governor.[10] That kind of compliment had not worked for the Pottingers previously, however, and it would prove just as inadequate once again. The Pottingers were stubbornly resolute, a quality eminently suitable to the great, but it did mean they sometimes failed to heed the lessons of the past. The flattery had ended badly in the instance of Walter Raleigh and Charles Fox; and now again, for baby Eldred Elphinstone died in his infancy, just short of his second birthday. The Pottingers never succeeded in winning an advantage from blarney. They were meant to make their own way.

Henry applied himself to his magisterial duties, and his collecting duties – checking on the revenue officers – with rigour and applied diligence. He most certainly would not put himself under an obligation to grant favours, the common course of conduct in India. He remained stern and aloof, so much so that the Governor saw fit to caution him, about both his temper and his manner:

> If you will allow yourself to be put out of temper ... you will soon frighten them [the peasant community] from your presence, and will be at the mercy of the people about you who know your real disposition, and who will take pains to give false impressions of it to others. If you really had a bad temper it would be needless to remonstrate, but it is a pity to sacrifice the advantage of a good one to a habit of giving way to provocation.[11]

The Governor, as we know, had his own back story; there was more than one side to him. He may have presented in public as mild and ecumenical, setting aside when he was conducting a battle, but here it is apparent that he had a mistrust of those 'others', those with whom he went to battle no doubt. It can hardly be a surprise that Pottinger should have followed his lead in that.

On the other hand, we can understand this assertive confidence differently. It was incumbent on him to make sure that the community should understand the standards of behaviour expected of them. They should know right from wrong, and Henry would ensure it. It is another example of the inherent greatness of the man breaking through. Elphinstone was surely wrong to have chastised him, however gently. He had failed to recognise who he was dealing with.

Unfortunately, Henry had usurped a position customarily the preserve of civilian officers of the Company, whereas he was from the military side. He was not a good fit in this role. The Governor should have thought of that. Whatever Elphinstone's rationalising, in short order he appointed his protégé to a new role, the Resident at Kutch.

But first, there had to be a residence for the Resident. In May 1825, Henry moved into a sprawling bungalow outside the principal town, remote and dusty Bhuj, with typical wide-trellised verandahs and tiled roof, large landscaped grounds – lawns (such as survived in the semi-desert conditions of that part of the world) and hedges, grand driveway and an admittedly modest picket gateway. Strategically located close to the Bhuj fort, where the British forces were stationed, it was also on the road out to the coast, in case of awkward necessity.[12]

Here he set himself up as a spymaster. He had learned from Elphinstone the importance of being informed in advance. His own network of agents brought back a stream of secret reports on what the amirs were up to, for Pottinger was now that much closer to Sindh, and his brief was to keep his eye upon them. Soon he had assistance – from the Burnes brothers: Alexander, who would become the next rising star of the northwest, and James, an army doctor and mysteriously important in freemasonry.

Like Pottinger, they too were intent on making their way in the world. They had no need to draw on their connection to their distant cousin Robbie, the ploughman poet. The wider Scots connection, though, seemed to stand them in good stead – Malcolm, Elphinstone, Minto – the higher echelons of the Company were full of them. When not on various tours of duty, the Burnes brothers were based in the massive hill fort.

In keeping with his new importance, Pottinger was promoted to major. As he had benefited from the supervision of Elphinstone and Malcolm, so now in his turn he passed on the courtesy, seconding in 1827 the nomination of Alexander Burnes to the Bombay Literary Society.[13] He was learning something: *noblesse oblige*. He went further, he pushed the case for Burnes to be chosen for what was essentially a reconnoitering mission into the territory of the nefarious amirs in Sindh. A plan had been concocted to take a gift of large dray horses up through that country and into the adjoining lands of the Sikhs, a present for their maharajah, Ranjit Singh. That was cover for the real purpose, which was once again to map the Indus.

And to pre-empt the amirs refusing to permit passage up the river (arguing that horses should be able to walk), Henry Pottinger devised a stratagem. There should be an enormous carriage for the horses to pull, which of course would have been shaken to pieces before it arrived at Ranjit Singh's court, which would mean it had to be ferried up the river, a slow enough undertaking for the British to take as many soundings as they needed, to track the main channels through all the shallows and sandbars. It was a means of getting the British into hostile territory. It was in effect another version of the Trojan horse, and Pottinger the wily Ulysses of this duplicity. A spymaster indeed. As a ruse, it was no more preposterous than the Greeks' classic fabrication.

When the amirs stalled the approval and continued to block the passage of the British, Pottinger did what he did best. He bullocked his way through the diplomatic impasse. The amirs, he reminded them in a thunderous letter, should remember how vulnerable they were to invasion by both the Sikhs and the Afghans, and they would do well to cooperate with the British. A different order of invasion, perhaps.

In the event, the expedition turned out to be rather disappointing. The Governor-General aborted the mission as an unworthy subterfuge. Burnes was denied his moment of glory because the Indus was never going to be suitable for steam navigation, no matter how many surveys were taken. And the maharajah was underwhelmed because the huge horses refused to gallop.

Pottinger's part in it as instigator was awkward for him; and when, subsequently, Burnes actually did publish a much-admired chart of the Indus, and was celebrated for it, Henry was forthright enough to report that he disagreed with Burnes's overly optimistic estimation. He put his disagreement on record. It was absurd to claim the Indus was never fewer than 15 feet deep, even in the dry season. Pottinger knew that was untrue. No vessel with a keel could make its way up the river. It might lead to poor investment if his assistant's misrepresentation were not corrected; and the young upstart should be put in his place. Jealousy had nothing to do with the matter. Besides, he was now a lieutenant-colonel and Burnes a mere lieutenant. There is such a thing as a pecking order.

What Pottinger did manage in consequence of all the sudden new attention and exchange of strong advice too, no doubt, was to win a treaty with the amirs, by which they agreed to open up the river to British trade. The amirs maintained a proviso, however: the British were not permitted to live in Sindh, nor were arms or military supplies to be brought up the river. But now the Company had what it wanted, and so did the British powers. They had a natural border against incursions from the north. And the annexation of this new territory had begun. It was Henry's first great coup.

With it came a second great accomplishment, to have sired another son, another along the unquestionably, unfathomably great river of Pottinger family history. Back in Bhuj his wife Susanna had given birth to Frederick, in April, the hottest part of the year. April, the cruellest month. Another brother, Harry, would be born in Bhuj three years later, in 1834. Their older sister, Henrietta, had been born in 1829.

The nature of his job frequently called Henry away, for extended periods of time. That did not make for a close family. But it is also testimony that the great are not overcome by uxoriousness. Henry knew where his higher duty lay. As political events unfolded, he was required to spend not just months but in fact the better part of two years up the river in Hyderabad (not to be confused with Hyderabad in Telugu, the City of Pearls), cajoling and bullying the amirs to sign a new treaty of his devising, allowing traffic along the Indus, with reduced tolls. Then, all the while mistrusting them as habitual liars, he bustled them into giving permission for a garrison to be stationed there, to protect them and their favoured hunting reserves from the Sikhs and the Afghans. And finally, he negotiated the establishment of a Residency. He himself was, of course, the obvious choice to take up that position. His assistant, Alexander Burnes, had been extracted from Bhuj, the centre of the web, and was commissioned for an enterprise through the mountains and into what would prove a fatal struggle for Herat.

If Susanna were to be left behind in distant Bhuj all the while, why would she not take the opportunity to decamp?

The Cookes of Cooketown were evidently a lesser family. Susanna, fearful for her children after the early death of her first-born, and not especially enjoying the relentless heat, the aridity, the disease, took her children back to England to enjoy the rounds of a more genteel way of life. In the end though, wifely duty or one of Henry's booming letters reminded her where her obligation lay. She returned to India in 1839, assuaging her change of mind by sailing out as chaperone to two of her nieces, who had had an elegant sufficiency of practising their airs, not only on the spinet. They were now ready for the marriage market. She left her vulnerable children behind, however, in the tender care of relations.[14]

V

THE SORCERER'S APPRENTICE

Better not be at all than not be noble.

—ALFRED, LORD TENNYSON, *The Princess*

HENRY'S TWO LUCKLESS nieces, daughters of the impecunious Thomas – Tommy Teapots – were not the only Pottingers in circulation in India. Henry's younger brother William, for one, had joined the mission to Hyderabad in 1831; but much more prominent in the roiling flood of Pottinger greatness was Eldred, stepbrother of those nieces, eldest son of the ever-indigent Thomas, eldest grandson of the other Eldred. The first-born of the coming generation, like his uncle he had made his way to India to serve his country in the army, and after some years was transferred to the political department, working with his uncle.

He admired Henry, properly so; and as imitation is the sincerest form of flattery, he modelled his own character and career upon his so successful kinsman. Earnest as Henry was earnest, intrepid as Henry was intrepid, brave as Henry was brave, and resourceful as Henry was resourceful, he copied all his uncle's essential attributes. He showed himself to be self-reliant when he went gathering intelligence, he proved adept at passing himself off as a native, both by his disguise and by his fluency in local languages. He showed his mettle in much the same manner as his uncle had, in much the same kind of mission. He hid behind a more than functional beard. He was his uncle's second self.

So we can think of him as a kind of anabranch to the family's historical river. A billabong, if you will. Only, that relates to a part of the world on which the Pottingers had yet to make their mark, and leave their trace.

This Eldred, like so many other Pottingers, had thought immediately of the Honourable East India Company as a prospective employer. That might have been an emerging family tradition, or it might have been that as a youngster he read his Uncle Henry's account of travelling incognito in Belochistan as the Company's secret agent. From whatever cause, he began his training at their newly established, and unfortunately named, Military Seminary at Addiscombe, in Surrey. Onward Christian soldiers?

Here, at the age of 14, he was enrolled for two years, to learn the requisite skills for pointing very big guns at a target, say an oncoming military force, and firing at it on command. He was learning to become an officer in the Company's army, learning the drill. Which meant not just remembering to stand well behind the cannon, but how to construct gun carriages, the science of fortifications, the mathematics of gunnery, and the art of drawing and surveying. The cadets there learned

French and Latin (useful should either Napoleon or Julius Caesar come again) and a modicum of Hindustani (for ordering the native troops about). And they learned to fight, fine-tuning their skills in the streets and markets of nearby Croydon.[1] Without sanction, of course, but boys will be boys. That too was useful later on in India.

The fees for this college were of the order of £50 a term – Eldred's father would have had to scrabble that together. The cadets always wore a green swallow-tailed uniform, a cheap uniform according to an unimpressed J.M. Bourne.[2] In this they attended classes and chapel, and made their sorties into town. Photographs from the era – at the dawn of that newfangled technology – show them to be less than spick and span, more rumpled.

Eldred fitted right into the academy, though his adoring biographer, Maud Diver, acknowledges that he was quick-tempered and hot-headed.[3] That would be his Irishness. And not too different from Uncle Henry, apparently. Or perhaps (as was to emerge) his cousin Fred.

At Addiscombe he displayed a surprising mechanical aptitude, possibly a surprise to himself too. For he experimented with the military hardware and invented a new kind of shell, and put it to the test. According to Maud Diver he:

> daringly exploded it, to the dismay of the authorities and the peril of those who shared the fun. Invention or mere mischief, there was good promise in either. But the significance of the incident lies deeper. Though others were implicated, Gentleman-Cadet Pottinger took on himself

> all responsibility for the breach of college rules, and tried to bear all the punishment. It went near to cost him his commission, yet nothing would induce him to reveal the names of his friends.[4]

We can see the thinking. If it were to turn out a splendid success, it would be well to corral all the praise and possible advancement. Purely a matter for speculation, of course. That episode was not quite as radical as the brief wild moment of insubordination at Belfast Academy, but potentially much more sensational. Uncle Henry would have honoured the intrepidity of it.

The niggling thought that the Pottingers did not readily share their moments of greatness is completely unworthy.

In 1828, having completed his four terms of training, Eldred was sent off to Bombay as a military cadet. That was closer to Henry's sphere of influence; and it is not impossible that Henry played a role in orchestrating a lucrative regimental staff situation. Those involved in artillery were in the thick of such skirmishes and battles, as broke out from time to time; and, indeed, in the thick of the looting and pillaging that invariably followed. We make no assumption that Eldred would have had any truck with such activity; and even if he did, he showed how truly honourable he was by requesting a transfer to a native cavalry unit or perhaps two irregular cavalry units, which was a less profitable post.[5] Horses, after all, and he was a Pottinger through and through.

It was always going to be a mere matter of time before Eldred was assigned to be an assistant to Henry at the Kutch

Residency. When that transpired, he embarked on missions to gather intelligence, sometimes covert. Now he was in the political wing. He too was a spy.

But perhaps not quite as wily as he needed to be. Sir John Kaye, the eminent historian of the Sepoy war in India, wrote a brief but revealing thumb sketch of the young man:

> One day Eldred appeared before his uncle in a great state of excitement, declaring he had been grossly insulted by a native – a horsekeeper, or some other inferior person – on which Henry Pottinger, amused by his young relative's earnestness, said, smilingly, 'So, I suppose you killed him, Eldred?' 'No' replied the young subaltern, 'but I will, uncle'. Thinking that this was an instruction from higher authority, he was quite earnest in his declaration. It need not be added that the joke exploded, and the retributive hand was restrained.[6]

Sir John, it must be observed, was *parti pris*, for it was he who would write the story of Eldred's subsequent heroics. Here was early evidence of what was to come. Kaye admired that intense application to the sense of what was properly due to the British, just as much as Uncle Henry's patriotic self-awareness in Balochistan and elsewhere. Good order must prevail, and lesser beings should know their place. It was all quite simple, really: there were those who rode horses, then there were the horses, and then those who tended them. A natural hierarchy, and perhaps not too far from a caste system either. Certainly, there was no sympathy for those who would attempt to disturb it. Was it too much to demand respect?

Like his uncle, Eldred volunteered (this in 1836) for a potentially dangerous mission, but an important one nevertheless, to undertake surveys of the precipitous mountain passes to the northwest of the Indus – for the momentum was gathering. It had been inevitable that at some stage the British would lead a vast army into what is now modern-day Pakistan. They were no longer apprehensive of Napoleon's eagle; now they were suspicious of the Russian bear.

Only, Eldred was hampered by a local war, and although he was safely ensconced in amongst a body of Sindh Irregular Horse, and even more safely disguised as a horse dealer, a variant kind of irregularity, he could not proceed with his mission. That disguise is one we have come across already, the preferred disguise of his elder kinsman.

Eldred and Burnes, both working for Henry, caught up with each in Kabul, having made their way there through separate mountain passes. Eldred was in an awkward position, for he did not have Burnes's diplomatic credentials. After a few anxious months he decided to flee the city, lest he be detained there.

And this is how and where greatness manifests itself. By sheer good chance, or magnificent coincidence, Eldred chose to make his way to Herat. He could have gone anywhere; but as fate decreed, the kind of fate that attends those who are marked out for greatness, he happened to be exactly where he was needed, just as the Persian army with its Russian military advisors also arrived and set a siege in place.

Here, Eldred Pottinger achieved his claim to fame. For by report, he saw – and he was aghast at what he saw – how dispirited the defenders were, how inept and indecisive their leaders were, how spineless. And he took it upon himself to lead the resistance. He determined where best to position the few riflemen at his disposal, he berated their chief, and even – so it is said – beat him back to a breach in the barricade with the flat of his sword when the *wazir* – the local administrator – tried to flee. And his efforts paid off magnificently. The attacking forces were fended off, the siege dragged on and eventually sputtered out, the Persians withdrew and he had singlehandedly brought that about. Eldred was the 'hero of Herat', he was thanked by the Governor-General, he was promoted for his effort, he was knighted, and he was appointed the political officer in Herat. He was celebrated in the papers back home, his portrait was drawn and reproduced everywhere. Another magnificent Pottinger.

One of the first pictures of Eldred is of him in uniform, sitting at the side of a cannon, calmly looking out at whatever proceedings were afoot, or not, as the case may be. His cloak is slung nonchalantly off one shoulder, reminding us that it was cool if not cold up there in the mountains, on the battlements. One foot – a delicate foot, let it be said, suggesting the artist who happened to be there at the time was more familiar with dancing pumps than officers' boots – an elegant foot rests on a little pyramid of cannon balls. These, it will please you to know, were commonly stacked inside a brass monkey – a perimeter of the bottom layer – and if, because of the freezing cold, it contracted sufficiently, then the iron balls would tumble down. That is a much less vulgar explanation of a common expression, and one likely to be encountered in experiences of extreme winter chill.

Other portraits appeared too, with Eldred in native guise, his curly black hair nearly hidden under his turban, his eyes variously black or light blue, his nose either snubbed or long, his face somewhat expressionless or, more kindly, impassive. He had not quite mastered Henry's commanding presence.

Meanwhile, a separate battle of slow attrition was continuing in and from the Bhuj Residency. Henry Pottinger had on a number of occasions demurred from Alexander Burnes's reports, which mostly were channelled through his office. Burnes was not one to take that unflinchingly. He had let it be known to 'higher up' that he thought Henry had abused his authority against the local ruler. Burnes was ever more inclined to liberal views about Indian government, Pottinger instinctively more authoritarian, defensive of British interests. Burnes referred to him as a bully. Pottinger complained of this move 'to blacken and ruin my public character'.[7] We might note that Burnes, who was lionised for his public character, would be ruined by his own private character. It was all a bit tense between them.

Then they fell out over as serious an issue as the landing of the Bombay army on its way to join the Grand Army of the Indus (whereby Britain would seize Afghanistan, ostensibly to save it from a fate worse than death). The troops from Bombay were to sail up to Karachi and disembark there. Burnes had planned it all. But this was Pottinger's particular fiefdom, and he would not be bypassed. He forbade what might be misinterpreted as an invasion of Karachi and insisted instead that the British troops be landed at a distance from there, where they had to await the arrival of their baggage animals by land, from Kutch. Pottinger intervened too in the matter of their route to the rendezvous with troops from Calcutta – Burnes had mapped a feasible route across the Thatta desert, more or less a straight line. But Pottinger remembered that country and directed the army to proceed by a much longer route around the edge of the desert.

Again we must be careful. Anyone might think the worst of him, finding a way of countermanding Burnes's orders, a means of subverting his plans. That is just petty, and reflects badly on those who, smaller-minded, think that way. For it is plain for all to see that he was being careful about the sensitivities of the peoples in that region, and he was taking care to preserve the army intact, so that it might be fighting fit when the time came for it to confront the enemy – whichever enemy that might be. Rather than criticise our colonel, we should admire his caution and his foresight. That, after all, was precisely consistent with the frame of mind of the military leaders. Never mind that the delay complicated the invasion, and the crossing of the Indus. And never mind that the grounds for the British advance – the siege by the Persians of Herat – had by this time disappeared. Pottinger was clearly attuned to their *modus operandi*.

In any case, if he were crossing swords with one who had been his all but insubordinate subordinate, it would have been ignominious for him not to stand his ground. The Company demanded it. Hierarchy must prevail. Order and control had to be maintained.

Once across the great river, to the screel of pipes and the thump of drums, the combined force advanced over arid desert country, over plains rising towards the famous mountain passes, including the Bolan pass, which Eldred had surveyed, but avoiding the Khyber Pass, which would have exposed them to the formidable Sikhs. Unfortunately, because of the circuitous route the Bombay contingent had taken, and because of its late arrival, the delays meant very little of their stores caught up with them. The men had to struggle up those heights with heavy packs. There was drought and famine. Sniper fire accompanied them along the way, and potent ambushes.

The Pottingers were well outside this military straggle, one keeping to home base and corresponding with Lord Auckland, the other on base at Herat, sending his reports down to the approaching army. Henry was not happy; yet he was accomplishing one of his best results. He drafted a treaty with the Sind amirs, and this time achieved their signatures as the vast force trampled through their lands. He had enormous bargaining power, the visible threat of compulsory takeover. The amirs backed down one after the other and the British were conceded the access they had all along hankered for. Through this, he established the terms by which the British would keep their flag in the expanded territory, permanently opening up the Indus as they had always desired. In quite another sense that was to be his signature effort.

But he felt a strong sense of grievance. He wrote this out in an incautious, 11-page letter detailing his complaints about Alexander Burnes, his junior's insolence in criticising his, Henry's, despatches, or in acting on the Governor-General's instructions to him, Henry, before they had even reached his Residency. It was quite another matter that he had criticised Burnes's despatches. He was after all Burnes's superior, and not only was it proper for him to attach his assessment, but indeed it was his responsibility to do so.

This was not the first time he had objected to Burnes's pushing himself forward. Indeed, once he had gone so far as to threaten to resign. Lord Auckland's secretary expressed his Excellency's sorrow that matters had come to such a pass; and accepting the gist of what Henry had presented, tactfully regretted that Henry's health had been so impaired by the weight of his duties. He was granted leave to proceed to Bombay to recover his health. Which rather forced the issue, for a man has his pride. Henry tendered his resignation on 29 January 1839.[8]

Somewhere in amongst all this correspondence, it must have been pertinent that Henry's wife Susanna was on her way to Bombay, together with the nieces. When the ladies eventually reached the khaki environs of Bhuj, Henry's resignation had not yet come into effect. It would have had to be considered by the Court of Directors of the East India Company, back in Leadenhall Street, London; and then ratification sent out to Calcutta, and so on to Bombay.

With the ending of his responsibilities in the Political Department of the East India Company, he turned his attention to matters of personal moment. Packing his uniforms and cummerbunds and 30 years worth of mementoes into trunks, he decided to return not to Ireland but to England, which might be seen as a tactful hint that he was a Company man through and through. And England, after all, was where further honours might be achieved. Also, that is where the most important investitures were held.

Once the Governor-General's endorsement was approved, the Pottingers began the requisite farewells, starting with Henry's senior in Poona. From there they travelled to Bombay by train. That was much more acceptable than the dusty road. And from there they travelled by way of Suez, which inconveniently did not yet have its canal. That meant an uncomfortable transfer to Alexandria, where their ship was delayed by an outbreak of plague, one that did not make it into the Biblical catalogue. It was, however, a cautionary reminder of what could happen at the lower end of a river, the opposite end of the springs of greatness.

And so back to England by sea – Port Out, Starboard Home – for Henry to recover his health. Very posh, Sir Henry and his lady. They did not arrive back in England until early 1840. In April he was formally created a baronet. He applied for a coat of arms, of course. How pleased the ancestors would have been. To emphasise his awareness of the sacrifices he had made over the years, he devised a shield with a squadron of pelicans arranged about a golden crown, the flecks of blood showing on their breast. *Virtus in ardua* indeed.

Pelicans, though, are considered to represent modesty. Three of them might be thought an overstatement.

The crown was an ambitious touch. Maybe to do with the sovereigns of Dublin, if not Alfred himself; although it is an eastern crown, hinting at that long service in the subcontinent. The green background was for Ireland, of course.

Evidently the design was not thought controversial, for the College of Arms approved it in July.[9]

You see? Of course this was a great man in the making. His country knew it. Well, officialdom then.

The rest of the Pottinger clan were undoubtedly proud of what Henry and Eldred had accomplished. A letter from Thomas (remember him?) to the President of the Board of Control had petitioned for recognition of Henry for that sterling service, for accomplishing the opening-up of Sindh and the Indus in particular, successfully negotiating with the amirs; and for Eldred for his reported heroics at Herat. He itemised how many Pottingers had served in India, how many had been killed and how many were still serving (as though that somehow contributed to the achievements of Henry and Eldred). No doubt that did steel their resolve but would not in itself count as their own attainment, as Thomas should have known; but it did not hurt to spruik the Pottinger pedigree. He rounded off his letter with:

> Under all these circumstances I look with confidence to Her Majesty's Government to confer the rank of Baronet on colonel Pottinger and on Eldred Pottinger the defender of Herat.[10]

Two baronetcies! That was possibly a bit of overreach. Thomas might have done well to have learned strategy from his brother, Henry.

Henry, knighted 10 June 1839, was not indifferent to something more in the way of honours. If a man is incipiently great, he should know his own worth. That much goes without saying.

And as in life, so in the best organised chronicles of lives, and even more unfailingly in the lives of the great – when one chapter closes, another opens.

Meanwhile, up in the vast reaches of the great frontier, the chief political strategist in this insurgence into Afghanistan, one William Macnaghten, took it upon himself to rein in the British expenditure on this foolhardy operation by halving the money that was paid to local chieftains so as to keep the mountain passes open. Those warlords were not only unhappy, they were shocked by such a breach of established protocol.

That was not impossibly the very sort of action Henry Pottinger might have initiated, had he been chosen for the role; but he would certainly not have made Macnaghten's next mistake, which was to accept an invitation by the chieftains to discuss the matter over a cup of tea. Macnaghten was shot dead as he dismounted, too trusting by far. That was not Pottinger's way.

With Macnaghten's assassination, the man to replace him was Eldred Pottinger, newly arrived – or rather, escaped – from Kohistan, where he had unimaginatively repeated himself by leading yet another resistance against insurgent tribesmen, adversaries rather more committed than the desultory Persians had been at Herat.[11] The means of his escape on this occasion, with a fellow officer, was by passing through the enemy lines, addressing the guard in Persian. When he reached Kabul, he had a bullet in his leg (not, apparently, fired by the guard). His fellow officer had lost a hand and was wounded in the back and the neck.

Eldred's wound was a blessing in disguise. When the Afghans rose up against the British in Kabul, murdering

Burnes for his shameful, shameless outrage of Muslim morality,[12] Eldred negotiated the terms and conditions of the British retreat down the Khyber Pass and was among those left behind as hostages. In all likelihood he would have been held anyway, but hampered as he was by his wound, it was less difficult to reconcile himself to his fate. He survived the harsh winter and then another five or six months beyond that in appalling conditions, until liberated by the returning 'Army of Retribution'. Virtually the entirety of the original British force, and their wives and servants and the native troops who had accompanied them, had been wiped out or froze or starved, their arms and stores looted, their horses taken. He survived where they did not.

Eldred was left languishing in India, to recover his health as well as he could. Just quietly, he was miffed that he had won no honours whatsoever for his troubles. The mystique of greatness was not on him. Henry had apparently quit the service as well as the field and was no longer at hand to push his cause. What could he do now?

For starters, Eldred would have to endure a court martial, an enquiry into the disaster of Kabul and the Khyber Pass.

VI

A PUFF OF SMOKE

With these celestial Wisdom calms the mind ...

—SAMUEL JOHNSON, *Vanity of Human Wishes*

NOT EVERYONE WAS enthralled by Henry's investiture as a baronet. Patently they did not grasp the essential greatness of the man.

The grand event took place on 27 April 1841, Frederick's birthday. Henry and Susanna had reclaimed their children, and not least Freddy, at this stage only nine years old and heir apparent to Henry's title. With his retirement from the East India Company, this was intended to be a time for Henry to recuperate; and the bestowing of that title soothed his ruffled feathers. It is only fitting for the inherently great to have a proper estimation of themselves, and that the world at large should acknowledge it.

Notably, Henry had not looked to return to Belfast. London was more his ambition.

Yet even as all this good will and occasional ill will was in circulation, in the Far East matters were unfolding. Henry had had his doubts about the treatment of the amirs in particular.

Not his treatment of them, their treatment by others. He had merely brought them into line.

In his opinion, Britain had not behaved honourably in forcing the opening of the Indus to commerce. But he created no public scandal about such matters. And his impeccable record as a formidable negotiator was now being recognised and appreciated by the government. He had served rather more predictably than Alexander Burnes, the show pony of the Afghan heights; and what Henry accomplished had proved less costly. Also less disastrous. If only they had listened to him instead of to Burnes. That shameless fellow had been too indulgent with what should have been kept tucked under his kilt, for Burnes had participated enthusiastically in the pleasures of the mile high club. That was the pitch at which he had lived and amused himself; and died. Just look at how he ended up. That is what happens when a man's reach exceeds his grasp.

Henry, on the other hand, knew exactly how to deal with subservient peoples, those who were about to be conquered. They respected their superiors, they respected those who spoke their mind clearly and frankly. And fearlessly.

It was unfortunate, of course, that in Bhuj, just before he resigned, locals had begun throwing bricks and stones at him.[1] Nothing more than an accident of timing, it was not the cause of his leaving the service. It had nothing whatsoever to do with his resignation; but it had kept him close to home while matters unfolded in Kabul and down – or up – the Khyber Pass.

Back in London, in the House, in the corridors of power, in the papers, there was massive discontent about all of that – about the overthrow of British interests in Kabul, not about

Pottinger. Britain had been humiliated; and now the news was no better from China, where a fortune in merchandise had been impounded and destroyed. This was all totally unacceptable. Matters were getting out of control, and those foreign regions should be made to know their place. In the case of Kabul, a huge and vengeful army (the 'Army of Retribution') stormed into the mountain vastnesses and wreaked extraordinary damage. China presented another problem altogether.

For what the Chinese authorities had just destroyed was about £20,000,000 worth of opium. It was of little moment that this had all been smuggled into China, a prohibited import. That was not the point. The point was that the opium trade was the means by which the British obtained the wherewithal to buy tea from China, and from which the Honourable Company derived massive profits when that delectable was in turn sold from the London warehouses. And the duty paid on this tea amounted to 10 per cent of the government's entire revenue.[2] Everybody had a vested interest – even the Chinese, who wanted to sell their tea.

But the Celestial Empire had grown most unhappy with the widespread addiction to pipe dreams. A commissioner was appointed to put a stop to the unhealthy trade, a Governor Lin, who had successfully eliminated the opium habit in his home province. Execution proved an effective guarantee against further lapses. Lin was expected to maintain a strong stand against this execrable commodity, and he did. In 1839 he even sent a letter of protest about the immorality of it to Queen Victoria, though it appears she never received his disapproving missive – not necessarily because it was mislaid in the post.

The Emperor sent Lin to Canton, where various British traders ('the barbarians') had established their depots, and where the vast bulk of opium was stored, awaiting transhipment. Effectively, this vast smuggling operation exposed the British as contrabandits, given that the importation of opium had been prohibited. But because on the last leg the goods were actually taken ashore by Chinese lighters, the traders were able to satisfy themselves that they had observed the letter of the law. They had not actually breached the embargo, because their direct involvement ceased out at sea.

A Captain Elliot was the nominal superintendent of this activity, on the British side. His commission was to gain access to other Chinese ports, so that the British might increase their trade in general. Obviously involvement in opium was unlikely to impress the local authorities, and eventually – for he privately thought the trade was unethical – Elliot agreed to Governor Lin's demands that the opium stocks held in the warehouses at Canton should be handed over. That might mollify the Chinese, and show the British as law-abiding. Who could ever have doubted it?

But what was handed over was immediately destroyed, mixed with water and lime and washed out to sea – 20,000 large chests of it, each weighing something like 150 pounds. That was a lot of opium.

The British traders were furious, and none more so than the leaders in that activity, the firm of Jardine Matheson. They were not so concerned with ethics as with the sacrosanct principle of free trade; and they wanted reparation for their impounded goods. The suspicion that they were protesting at any constraint on their enormous profits is a mere quibble, an unworthy thought. Of course they understood the Chinese regulations in this matter. But there are two sides to every story, and sometimes more.

And here we make a detour. In narratives such as the present one, essentially picaresque in character, it is customary to allow for a seemly digression from time to time. Lives are not tidily structured as they are in fictions. Yet when we review the whole, then we see what we didn't see before – how all sorts of incidental events have a bearing on outcomes that could not have been foreseen at the time. We are able to make out a pattern, we can follow a line much as a tracker does. We can separate out the incidental and read the convergences and divergences for what they are, all contributing to what becomes a grand design, in this instance, the inspiring emergence of rare greatness.

William Jardine and James Matheson were two young Scotsmen who had made their way to the Far East, intent on building a fortune through trade; that, after all, is what the Orient was for. Because they were both second sons, their prospects at home were never going to be very alluring.

Jardine was born on a farm in Dumfriesshire in 1784; he was just five years older than Henry Pottinger. His father had died while he was not much more than a bairn. His older brother, who inherited the farm of course, supported him while he qualified in medicine, as so many young Scots seemed to do, especially in picaresque narratives. Tobias Smollett has much to answer for. Like Henry Pottinger, Jardine bound himself to the East India Company; more like Smollett, he sailed as a ship's surgeon.

The ancestral Jardines had come across the Channel with William the Conqueror – another of that mass of immigrating boat people, 'the staid, conservative, Came-over-with-the-Conqueror type ...'[3] And here once more is the uncanniness of how matters work out in the stories of the truly great. Here we are given what has so far been missing, a yardstick against which to appreciate the Pottinger attainment.

The Jardines' ancestral name was du Jardon, another family uprooting itself from the garden. Who can say, the two families may well have known each other once upon a time, extracting themselves from a common plot. The early Jardines settled in the midst of reiver country, the same country that had supplied so many settlers in Henry's native Ulster. Here they sensibly built a defensive fortress, Spedlins Castle, an uprighteously grim square tower with dungeons, more Robert Louis Stevenson than Walt Disney. The farm of William Jardine's unfortunate father was just nearby.

At some stage in the seventeenth century Sir Alexander Jardine had a falling-out with his miller, Dunty Porteous, and locked him in the basement cellar. Then he was called away to Edinburgh, a journey of the best part of a week. As he approached 'auld Reekie', he realised he still had the key to the dungeon in his pocket. Given the size of keys in the days of yore, that is not easily understood. Perhaps the laird had deep pockets. Irregardless, as our more enlightened politicians say, he sent back a servant with the key, and doubtless some direction about sustenance for the unhappy miller; but as it turned out, the servant was too late. The prisoner had died. And there were indications that he had gnawed at his own hand.

When the laird returned to take up his residence, alarming noises began to be heard from the cellarage. A ghost kept complaining of its hunger: 'Let me out – I'm deen of hunger!' And this was so persistent as to distress the family, to the extent that they called in a chaplain to exorcise the ghost. That was nearly successful. The unhappy wraith could be constrained to its cell by the presence of the family Bible. When the family moved across the river to a newly built Hall, they made the mistake of taking their Bible with them, for they found the only way to confine this unhappy visitant to its own proper haunt was to return the good book to a niche just outside the dungeon.

That was William Jardine's heritage. We might point to one particular mannerism of his, of gnawing his hand when he was considering some deep issue. We might notice too that he was lean and lanky, and his legs were rather thin, like Jack Sprat. This at a time when, following the fashion set by Beau Geste at the Bath pumphouse, it was considered *de rigeur* to present shapely shanks.

We are reminded yet once more how persistently the narratives of the great are associated with the remarkable. Alfred's apprenticeship in the kitchen of a Wessex hovel, Arthur's Tintagel and his Round Table, the storms and eruptions and earthquakes at the time of Julius Caesar's assassination ... of course it is not suggested that Jardine was in anything like that league. But he and his family make their own useful contribution to our investigation into the true measure of greatness.

Jardine was not one to indulge himself, nor anyone else. He had only one chair in his office. A visitor had to stand, as a means of keeping the interview brief and to the point. He had little in the way of conversation. He was single-minded in his application to his work. He despised idleness, and he had minimal time for society. He never married.

He retired from active trading in 1839 and returned to London, where he at once presented himself to the Foreign Secretary, Lord Palmerston. He wanted reparation for his lost opium. Palmerston knew that Britain had not the means to refund the merchants, and the only way to find that sort of money was to make China pay, which meant war. Jardine, hard-headed (he was known to the Chinese as 'rat with iron-head'[4] because he had walked away unruffled from an assault with a club in Canton), had all the maps and plans and strategies to hand, the numbers of troops and warships that would be needed. He laid out the desirability of an enforced commercial treaty, to open up further ports of trade; and he added the option of occupying Hong Kong, because of its anchorage and as a means of controlling the waterway to the Pearl River.

As an almost direct consequence of his knocking on parliamentary doors, committees met, speeches were made, orders were given and troops were despatched to commence engagements in what became known as the First Opium War. Hostilities began with their destruction of a blockade the Chinese had contrived in the river estuary, though some might well argue that it had begun with the confiscation and destruction of all that opium. Or they might argue that it had begun with the smuggling of the opium. That is of little significance in our narrative. Once they had ascended to Canton, Captain

Elliot, the superintendent, infuriated his superiors by negotiating a conciliatory treaty with China, which in the event neither side would ratify. He learned of his replacement only shortly before that replacement arrived – none other than the hero of the hour, Sir Henry Pottinger, swooping in just after some portentous typhoons. This was more the style of man Jardine had envisaged.

Sir Henry was appointed in May 1841, not by the Court of Directors of the East India Company, but by the Queen. The Honourable Company readily assented. He left England early in June – which meant very little time for consultation with the Foreign Office and such as William Jardine[5] – and, making an express passage to his new posting, arrived 10 August, at the height of the wet season, with all the discomfort and humidity that entailed. He had come via Suez by the overland route in the remarkably fast time of 67 days.[6] So quickly did he make his arrangements, he could not have been much encumbered by unwieldy quantities of baggage. Nor, for that matter, by a wife, family and entourage of servants. He had no intention of staying in the post for long. His commission was to take up a forceful engagement with China, in effect war, and to win it quickly. He was just the man to do it, Belfast-tough and a hands-on micromanager. His moment had come. He was about to meet his destiny.

We note here the acute instinct by which he was confirming the Pottinger lineage. He was to find his real destiny at the mouth of a great river, the issue of some distant ancestral spring. He had found his rightful place. True greatness cannot be denied.

Clearly he had made an impressive recovery in his limited retirement; and just as clearly, he was in no mood for shilly-shallying. His country required him to rise to the occasion. He barely paused to shake hands with Elliot before starting off from Hong Kong aboard a steam frigate, in hot pursuit of the British forces, which were just heading out up the China coast. He had no military command but he had sovereign political authority, and he was determined to be right on the scene of whatever happened.

The first objective of the British was Amoy, one of the ports they wished to force open to trade. As it happened, the display of force was more successful than any gunnery. British troops easily overran the city, which had been abandoned by all but looters. Thence to Chusan, where the expedition re-gathered after it had been dispersed by a gale. The northeast monsoon was settling in. Again the British forces, a different kind of storm, outmanoeuvred the Chinese; and so on to Ningpo, which surrendered without a shot being fired and which would provide suitable winter quarters.

Here Pottinger, well versed in the practices of the East India Company's military, fully expected his troops to reward themselves with some energetic looting. He was supported in this view by the admiral of the fleet, but not by the general commanding his troops. Well then, if pillaging was not acceptable, he could encourage the vigorous dismantling of public infrastructure and the enforced sale of goods (such as rice) to retrieve some of the costs of his expedition. A true hero, he was being careful of the public purse even while he was building pressure against the Imperial Court in Peking, to add weight to those impending negotiations, which must be the whole *raison d'être* for this operation. Pottinger would bring the Emperor to heel. In this he was much more forthright than had been Lord Macartney, who in 1793 had refused to kowtow to the Son of Heaven.

During the winter months Pottinger returned to Hong Kong, where much awaited to be done in terms of regularising arrangements. A mostly bald, barren rocky island, steep and hilly and at that time largely unpopulated, it had nevertheless a very desirable deep harbour – something of an oriental Gibraltar without the apes. At the time that Pottinger took over from Elliot, traders were already beginning to drift in with the turn of the tide, a kind of human flotsam and jetsam. Rudimentary warehouses, made mainly of woven matting, were starting to proliferate; they spread out along the waterfront and without necessarily a legal entitlement to their premises. Jardine and Matheson were among the first of the traders to relocate from the approved (and controlled) precinct at Canton. There were floating villages too, where the people made a bare subsistence from fishing, and from whatever other nefarious activities came to hand.

The climate was less than ideal. Through the warmer months the heat proved oppressive to the Europeans. They found it hotter than India. In the north of the island, in an area known as Happy Valley, malaria proved lethal. In the winter months the temperature dropped alarmingly. The flood gates of heaven opened, and early travellers reported that ice formed in water jugs overnight.[7] With the return of the warmer months, the rains ceased, only to be replaced by rising 'miasmata', and the unhealthiness returned. Such rapidity and frequency of change in the weather was not only trying, it frequently proved fatal.

And no birds sang.

Yet Pottinger continued to report glowingly about his coming fiefdom. Its secure and strategic location was eminently desirable; and he was confident that it would blossom too, and very quickly, as a centre for trade. He could see what others could not. Location, location, location.

When the warm weather returned, and further British troops arrived to man the garrisons they had established up along the coast – their success had been so swift that they were forced to spread their ranks thinly in order to secure their gains – Pottinger went aboard the steam frigate *Queen* again to join the squadron as it advanced further, easily securing Shanghai and then pushing up the Yangtze river and coming to anchor just outside Nanking. They were a formidable force; the rapidity of their progress was a great humiliation to the Chinese, and never to be forgotten.

The whole intent of their expedition was to bring Peking to the negotiating table. At Nanking, delegates approached the British to commence just such an arrangement. It soon became clear that the Chinese were stalling, and Pottinger moved into his fiercest and most forthright mode. He rejected every proposal they made. He wanted them to understand that he held all the military advantage, and he would have the treaty he wanted: 'to all his representations, the barbarian, Pottinger, only knit his brows, and said "No"'.[8] The Imperial Court had to understand that he would not be fobbed off. He meant business.

In consequence, a high-ranking official, Kiying, was appointed to negotiate the terms of what became known as the Treaty of Nanking, signed and witnessed aboard the *Cornwallis* on 29 August 1842. Pottinger had forced the issue: China would pay reparations for the opium that had been seized and destroyed; it would open five ports to foreign trade, with resident consuls; tariffs on imports and exports were to be moderate and uniform; and equality between officials of corresponding rank was to be recognised.

And then, in an overreach of his instructions, Pottinger also demanded that Hong Kong be ceded to Britain. This made for another difficulty, because with a recent change of Foreign Secretary he had been instructed to use the claim of the island only as a strategic bargaining tool. Whitehall did not wish to lumber itself with the cost of developing and sustaining a new colony. Not a word about that other awkwardness, the topic of opium, but then that would resolve itself as Hong Kong could serve as the distribution centre – which turned out to be the case.

At the ceremonial reception that followed, Kiying discovered an appetite for cherry brandy, and of course Pottinger would have been obliged to match him toast for toast. He had to, to preserve the honour of his Queen and country. If that required him to become a doughty trencherman, then he would do it.

He was startled, however, when Kiying requested him to open his mouth, whereupon the Chinese negotiator popped in a couple of sugar plums, claiming this was an old Manchurian custom denoting mutual confidence. That may be so, or it may have been mischief. Inscrutable. Either way, it is one of the rare occasions when our hero was left with his mouth gaping.[9] Or perhaps it was about discovering what he could manage with aplomb, though Kiying's translator might have had difficulty conveying that strained joke.

His political masters were delighted with both the outcome, and the energetic measures he had taken to achieve it. At the end of the year, he was made a Grand Commander of the Bath. This peculiar honour might in its turn have proved mystifying to the enigmatic Kiying.

In the months that followed, relations between the two countries improved, and Pottinger arranged a formal dinner with Kiying and his advisors after the ratification of the treaty, and presumably to celebrate his elevation to the governorship of Hong Kong (26 June 1843). This would have been held in a newly constructed Government House, built on one of the few level sites but with difficult access,[10] an elevated view over the harbour and with a lofty bald hill louring behind it.

The evening started out splendidly; Kiying was in great good humour, possibly because he knew something that Pottinger did not: that he had inserted some additional clauses into the Chinese language version of the treaty. As the two plenipotentiaries warmed to each other, so Pottinger subsequently reported to the Foreign Minister, the Earl of Aberdeen, and using his own spelling of the foreign dignitary's name:

> Keying's attention was attracted to the miniatures of my family which happened to be on the table, and he desired Mr Morrison [Pottinger's translator] to explain to me that

he had no son himself and therefore wished to adopt my eldest boy and to know if I would allow him to come to China. To this I replied that the lad's education must first be attended to, but that stranger things had happened than his seeing Keying. Hereafter to which His Excellency rejoined 'Very well, he is my adopted son from this day, his name – which he had previously ascertained – shall henceforth be Frederick Keying Pottinger and until you send him to me after he is educated you must allow me to keep his likeness.' To this proposal I could make no objection and I accordingly gave him the picture. Immediately His Excellency expressed a strong wish to have Lady Pottinger's miniature also, but ... before the matter was either way settled, dinner was announced and we went to table.

I supposed the thing would be forgotten, but when dinner was partly over, Keying again introduced his request, said that he would send me his wife's likeness in return, and that he wanted my whole family to take back with him when he went to Nanking and eventually to show to his friends at Peking. I felt it was impossible to refuse this flattering request, and I had the miniature brought and put it into his hands. He immediately rose, placed it on his head – which I am told is the highest token of respect and friendship – filled a glass of wine, held the picture in front of his face, murmured some words in a low voice, drank the wine, again placed the picture on his head and then sat down ... He then delivered the miniature to his principal attendant, who was standing behind him and directed him to send it home in his state chair.[11]

Clearly Sir Henry was equal to the moment; that is, he maintained his composure. It was certainly astonishing to him, and somewhat disconcerting to have this emissary all but abduct his wife and his son. Especially so as foreign wives, the wives of the barbarians, had been banned from entering China. We know Lady Pottinger was not present – why would Kiying request a portrait if she had been there? In fact, the press was reporting her presence in London society at the time.[12]

And Sir Henry was diplomatically evasive about fostering out his son and heir. In point of fact, there had been no intention of bringing his family with him. His mission was potentially much too dangerous for that and demanded his whole focus. Hong Kong was not like India, where Lady Pottinger had been able to play the grand lady to her heart's content. If Frederick's education was to be attended to, that would not happen in Hong Kong either.

Actually, there was very little in the way of genteel society to be enjoyed on the island, especially once the army had returned to India. Most of the people in the new settlement were shopkeepers and businessmen, or Portuguese from Macao. The number of those who existed for social purposes was quite limited; and of these there were few to whom he would wish to give the time of day.[13] He kept to himself, and his own small circle. He was inclined to think everyone else was mixed up in smuggling as much as trading, that they were involved with opium, and even that they were probably linked with some of the local activities of pirates.

The Chinese, in turn, were not flattered by his disdain for them. But then that is another of the hallmarks of greatness, to maintain one's own standards. To object to that is to display one's own small-mindedness.

In the absence of his family, and of much in the way of society, Sir Henry found solace in the company of 'pretty Mrs Morgan, fair, fat, and forty'.[14] She was the obliging wife of one of Jardine Matheson's captains, whom as a gesture of amity and esteem Sir Henry had appointed to serve as one of the new colony's Justices of the Peace.[15] Henry did not expect to encounter him much in that activity; and even less so in his maritime activity. The advantage there was that Morgan would be conveniently absent from time to time either on voyages back to India to pick up opium and other trade goods, or delivering the same up to the newly opened trading ports, further up the Chinese coast.

It would have been difficult for Sir Henry to be wholly discreet in such a small community. Not that this had been his style. He had seen the strategic advantage of a forthright attack, of storming the citadel – no side skirmishing. What was good enough for King Richard III was good enough for him. Besides, he was now the Governor: he was learning the potency of power.

The openness of the affair, however, was not so equably appreciated by that inferior sort of people, the merchants.[16] Besides, we might quite properly suspect that their disapproval was in fact supplementary to their disgruntlement with the regulations he was putting into place over their trading arrangements. And we must remember that the Pottingers had shaken themselves free of the cloying bog of that background. They had entered into an ascendancy. Consider it from Sir Henry's point of view. They were beneath his notice. Why should he care what they think? In fact, he would have contradicted his own standards had he taken any notice of them. Great man that he was, he could wish them to the devil, and be damned to them.

Quite possibly his private life was a little disturbed when, also at this time, his nephew Eldred, the 'hero of Herat', arrived from Calcutta, where there had been a requisite investigation (1 July) into his role in the recent catastrophic defeat of the British in Kabul. Eldred was exonerated, but he won no honours from his efforts. He had been wounded, and was still recovering; he had been imprisoned by the Afghans and was still recovering from that; and he was profoundly despondent. Also he had not arrived at a good time. This was a bad year for malaria – many of the troops who had come to fight the Chinese succumbed to the disease, as many as one in two, while among the local European population the rate was one in ten. Decimated, they were. The chief offensiveness of it came from open drains.

By the end of the year, Eldred, quite worn out, gave up the fight. He had accepted his uncle's offer of an appointment as temporary consul at Canton – kept him at a convenient distance from the steamy effusiveness of Mrs Morgan – but he was unable to take it up. In November he died, perhaps of what was called 'Hong Kong fever', though it has also been suggested more darkly that he may have committed suicide.[17]

Mrs Morgan was not in herself a sufficient enticement for Sir Henry to stay the course either, even though her husband had also succumbed to the fever, leaving her a relatively well-endowed widow. By this time she had an infant boy, baptised Henry William Herbert Morgan,[18] William being her late husband's name. That was undoubtedly an embarrassment. She was, according to Cree, a Bombay lady, an old acquaintance of Sir Henry's, but he leaves it open in what capacity he had known her formerly; or what bearing that may have had, if any, on his returning then to Britain.[19]

In October, as soon as the amendments to the Nanking treaty, the Treaty of the Bogue, had been signed, Henry had written (in July 1843) to the Earl of Aberdeen, offering his resignation. This, after all, had been the original arrangement with Aberdeen, that his was to be a short and vigorous tour of duty. He was not interested in governing a tinpot colony. His ambition was for something much grander, something much more palatial. His replacement did not arrive until the following May.[20]

VII

THE SWIRLING CAPE

I speak of Africa and golden joys.

—WILLIAM SHAKESPEARE, *Henry IV, Part 2*

HENRY LEFT THE Far East on 7 May 1844. While he was steaming home, he was made a member of the Privy Council. He missed a grateful nation's celebratory fireworks in Hyde Park and the Tower of London,[1] but on arrival in October he was welcomed with rapturous acclamation, especially in Manchester and Liverpool, where he was feted as the guest of honour at large banquets and dinners, where speeches were made, toasts were raised and healths were drunk. Splendid pieces of commemorative silver plate were handed over. He was presented with the freedom of the various cities – London, Edinburgh and Glasgow[2] – and reports of it all were published in the morrow's paper. What a wonder Sir Henry had accomplished for the country. He was escorted by the Earl of Aberdeen to Windsor to visit the Queen.

It might have been after these ceremonial highlights that his chaperon observed how very little interest Sir Henry had in politics, or not in the kind that absorbed the greybeards of Westminster; and further, it might have been hereabouts that the Earl allowed himself to mock Henry's County Down accent. Which was a bit of a cheek, given that the accent from his part of the world has its own notable individuality.

All that adulation, all the applause, all the huzzahs were quite heady. His wife joined him for many of these ceremonial accolades. On the evidence of a memorial prepared by his nephew, the late Eldred Pottinger, and submitted therefore on that unfortunate's behalf by a brother John, we learn that Susanna and her daughter Henrietta had been living in Jersey.[3] The sons, whom Henry hardly knew because they had they been living separate from him for so long, also made their appearance. Young Frederick had just commenced his years at Eton College (1844–47). He was thought to be a rather fine young fellow, as was his junior brother. The Pottingers, it might be said, had arrived; and to confirm it all Henry bought and furnished an impressive and seriously eminent house at 67 Eaton Place, Belgrave Square. The echo there of his son's expensive education was undoubtedly coincidental, but satisfying too.

In June of the following year, Parliament voted him an annual pension of £1500, which would have helped out with Frederick's fees. Because Henry had been awarded the Grand Cross of the Order of the Bath, he was now entitled to supplement his coat arms with supporters. These hardly added to the artistry of the existing design, but then coats of arms are not designed for the Royal Academy; rather, for coach door panels. On one side of the shield was a mandarin holding a furled scroll, impassive; on the other, an Indian foot soldier holding his rifle; and each looks somewhat anomalous. Henry's eye was for rare distinctiveness, not for the picturesque.

He gave speeches about the possibilities of trade to China, he wrote letters to the press, he corrected articles about himself. Wherever he went, he promoted the enormous trade advantages Britain would now enjoy in China. The fact that he had been the instrument by which these measures had become possible was of course acknowledged, as was only right and proper. He assured the cotton manufacturers their trade would be beyond imagining. And he was at pains to quash the unworthy rumours which began to circulate, that the agreement he had reached with Kiying was not as promising as first thought. For slowly it was emerging that the anticipated trade with China was indeed limited to just the one port, Canton. Those subsequent but unnoticed clauses prohibited Chinese trade with Hong Kong except through Canton, and so there was very limited trade through which the Chinese might pay for imports – other than through opium. That was less exciting for the manufacturers of Liverpool and Manchester.

Sir Henry outfaced his critics, as we would expect of a great man. Still, uncertainty entered the corridors of Westminster; and he was not raised to the peerage as some might have anticipated. How fickle were the weathervanes of Whitehall.

Privately, though, he must have returned again and again to the occasion when Kiying symbolically abducted both his wife and his son, seized the family jewels as one might say. It must have felt as though he had been somehow dishonoured. What would Kiying have done with the portraits – put them in his trophy cabinet? Inscrutably Oriental, as was the fiendish trick of the inserted clauses. And yet he had seemed such an open, jolly, friendly old soul. We can only shake our head and reflect philosophically that we prefer our great men to have an open and trusting mind.

A portrait of Sir Henry painted in the next year, in 1846, shows him to be a handsome devil, clean-shaven but with a ladykiller moustache, slightly protuberant and pouched eyes, hooded like those of an old roué. And it discloses just the hint of a paunch. Patently there had been little opportunity and little occasion for Henry to exercise, to ride a horse around Hong Kong, for example, and he was about to pass his prime – he was now 57 – though still burly with it. 'Sir Henry has, we understand, a fine head and a powerful frame', wrote the *Dublin University Magazine*. 'He is a first-rate horseman, and has always been fond of field sports ...'[4] but equally that article remembered the strength of his celebrated Arab steed Bandicoot, an eight-year-old which had saved his master's life, carrying him, 'no light weight',[5] to safety.

It would have been unwise to put Sir Henry out to pasture just yet; and he was still hopeful of something more. Late in September, he agreed to accept an appointment as the next governor of the Cape colony. This was a Crown appointment, outside the East India Company's jurisdiction. That could not have been altogether agreeable to his wife, Lady Susanna. She declined to accompany him. Frederick was in middle school at Eton, his younger brother Harry would be enrolling in the following year, and his sister Henrietta would in two months turn the very interesting age of 17, which meant of course that she should remain in London to be presented at Court when the time came. These concerns were of the highest importance, and a long way from the troubles in China, not to mention those other vexatious reports of a potato famine in Ireland.

It did not take Henry long to determine the issue. He sailed on his own – with the usual retinue of personal staff of course, but also with Sir George Berkeley, who was to take command of the British forces in the colony – and was installed on 27 January of the following year. Henry had negotiated that he might also have as his private secretary Richard Woosnam, who had served him in that role in Hong Kong.

Lady Pottinger seems to have retained her composure over the inescapable separation, as is to be expected of the consort of such a distinguished man.

Henry left behind too his son and heir, young Frederick, who was on the way to becoming a strapping lad. Eton was intended to imbue young fellows with the attributes of a scholar and a gentleman. Given that Frederick had inherited the mantle of greatness and wore it with pride, he was not likely to have submitted meekly to the Eton custom of fagging – though that was a servility he was quite prepared to accept from smaller boys when he ascended into the fifth form. Frederick was designed by nature to make use of the famous playing fields, where a previous generation of boys had practised for the Battle of Waterloo – in actuality, more often muddy meadows and slippery tracks on foggy evenings. Besides, what benefit could all that Latin and Greek be to him? One desirable outcome though would have been smoothing out his father's unfortunate accent.

Eton was a place riddled with all sorts of quaint customs. It was organised on the basis of three terms a year, but called halves, which reflects the low importance attached at that time to the mathematics curriculum. As the first half finished in mid-December, Frederick had been released just in time to join his parents at that splendid banquet in the Liverpool town hall. Given Eton's customary miserable fare, the steady procession of courses on that occasion would have been gratefully appreciated by a growing boy.

For Eton offered somewhat spartan conditions in the first part of the 1840s. There were few washstands and basins, for example, and little in the way of study facilities – an insufficiency of desks and a negligible library. The great dormitory, the Long Chamber, built back in the days before the Pottingers had begun their long march to greatness, was dark and gloomy, the ceiling vastly high, and the wind whistled through its broken windows. Over 50 boys huddled together there through the long nights, locked in from 6.30 in the evening, to regale themselves with rat hunts, blanket tossing and simple bullying.[6] The oak floors accumulated dirt tramped in from the aforementioned playing fields. There were no masters in residence, or not just there; and senior boys kept what order they would, or not, as whim dictated, and were licensed to use a cane to enforce whatever they decreed.

This was not squalor, it was just the sort of place in which potential greatness could forge itself and make itself known. Midway through Frederick's enrolment at the college, though, the Long Chamber was reconfigured, the provision of food improved somewhat, and the boys' experience was no longer such a version of durance vile.[7] Fagging continued nonetheless.

Games were the great release for the boys. The leaders amongst them, the senior students, were almost young men. As Frederick was somewhat above-average height for his age, he showed to advantage in the famous Eton Field Game, charging with authority into packs of players, shouldering opponents aside, tackling vigorously, all in rehearsal for his coming manliness, all in celebration of physical prowess. With his build, he was a natural bully, but we should not let the accident of terminology misdirect our understanding.

He could jostle with the best of them, and must have given as good as he got if anyone dared kick him in the shins. He had his father's fierce temper; the Pottingers did not readily accept opposition. By which we mean that he was not unnecessarily rough in his play, but committed rather to making his presence felt and to assisting his comrades. That was where he could excel. We might note that a set of rules for this extraordinary game was not formulated until the very year Frederick left Eton. That is to say, players such as he were at liberty to enforce some sort of agreed pattern of play by their own prowess. It was indeed a proving ground for our coming hero.

Students might hire a horse from time to time, to ride about the countryside. It was only a short walk across the river to Windsor racecourse too, and given the Pottinger penchant for horse riding, young Frederick had plenty of opportunity to keep his interest lively. There was any amount of stable gossip where the masters kept their horses too. Royal Ascot was not far away, and horse racing took place across the river, though everyone knew that the river itself, the Thames, was out of bounds. It is to be remarked how once again a significant river courses both actually and metaphorically through the Pottinger story.

Henry was not present to witness his son's triumphs. He took up his post in South Africa in the high summer of 1847: he was installed in Cape Town late in January, but then two weeks later hastened to the embattled eastern frontier, to Grahamstown, arriving there at the end of February. A reporter for a local newspaper unkindly described him as 'somewhat stout', with thinning hair, and with a thoughtful look on his face.[8]

Sir George Berkeley had been appointed to command the troops because Sir Henry did not hold a commission in the British army. In fact Henry was now caught up in a kind of replay of his time in Hong Kong. He had authority but not military authority; he had a war to attend to, and then a settlement to impose; and his activities took him away from what would normally have been his base.

Government House had been prepared for his reception at Cape Town, but he did not choose to stay long – it was not grand in the manner of, say, Madras or Calcutta, though neither was it as modest as his former residence in Hong Kong. And Table Mountain towered up rather more vastly, and more ruggedly, than the steep hill behind his previous lodging.

No, a thorough professional, Henry turned to the business at hand, or rather, the business that awaited him elsewhere. That is another mark of his intrinsic greatness. Besides, there was a promise attached to his acceptance of the task his government had asked of him: when he had resolved the issues that were provoking unrest among the native peoples in Eastern Cape province, and when he had managed to settle everything down, then if an appointment should come up in India he would be considered for that.

Which might go some little way to explaining why Lady Pottinger had been so cool about shipping out to the Cape. For the expectation was that the incumbency of a governorship should be for a term of six years, and with the possibility of a second position in India to follow but with no certainty exactly where, she was disinclined to disturb the life of pleasure and genteel society to which she had become accustomed.

Henry turned his attention doggedly to the unruly mishmash of colonial disorganisation, as he found it, with tensions about land ownership and cattle raids and occasionally deadly fighting between the various tribes, the Boers and the troops who had here, as elsewhere, determined on a policy of establishing peace by force. Indeed, there were also tensions between the Dutch and the English, between the volunteers and the regular forces, between paid and unpaid conscripts, between those who were reasonably well fed and those who were not. Sir Henry understood all that. He had seen it in India and in China and he would be every bit as vigorous in establishing the rule of law here too, dammit. He was not one to mince matters. And why should he not take advantage of his prior experience? It had worked there, and would again. It was called colonising, and it is what he did best.

At the same time, he had to keep reminding Sir George that he, Sir Henry, was the Governor, and it was for him to determine policy and procedure. He held a commission to settle and adjust the affairs of the territories in South Africa. Sir George did not have the good sense to appreciate that, nor Henry's acknowledged expertise in all such matters. And his gout was playing up, which did not assist his temper. Henry's, that is. Sir George could look after himself.

For occasional relaxation, there was all that delightful South African wine to relish, and quite close to hand too. Furthermore, there was always some kind of social activity gravitating about the governor's residence, just as in Hong Kong. No Mrs Morgan perhaps, but whispers began to circulate here as there. Some years after the event it was reported in a Cape Town newspaper – pseudonymously, of course – that Sir Henry was a man 'who enjoyed his glass and his lass, smoked his cigar and took things easy'.[9] The letter appeared over the name 'Tancred', which was a nod towards Benjamin Disraeli's novel (1847). The allusion remains enigmatic, but points towards the lack of good faith in which Sir Henry found himself mired. But that is also where Disraeli wrote his inherently ambiguous remark, 'The East is a career' – ever so pertinent to Sir Henry's path.

The war with the Kaffirs, which his predecessor, Sir Peregrine Maitland, had declared all but over, was anything but, as the new Governor immediately discovered. Military actions had been sadly bungled, the population at large was seriously disaffected, the strategies that had been put in place were as poorly designed as they had been carried out.

If ever a set of circumstances cried out for an inspiriting leader it was here.

Sir George could agree with that, but had a different candidate in mind. After all, when it came to top brass, who better than he?

The Xhosa people, the so-called Kaffirs, were conducting a very effective guerilla war against the insurgent white settlers and other native peoples whom the Europeans were using as a kind of buffer. They stole cattle, they slaughtered cattle, they attacked farms and burned them, they set light to crops and to grass, they hid in well-covered country and ambushed patrols of soldiers and police and mutilated the dead. Sir Henry, noting that they were well armed and with no shortage of ammunition, forbade any trade with 'the enemy'. That was treasonable, that could be tried by court martial, and a guilty party could be shot.

This was the Henry of old. He had lost none of his no-nonsense decisiveness.

He was dismayed that Sir Peregrine had abolished martial law and had sent the burghers, the Dutch colonists, back to their homes. There was a serious confrontation to be won. He called them up again, they were discontented and within a week or two of – as it seemed – ineffective pursuit of elusive tribesmen, they disbanded to return to their unprotected homes, claiming they had been told they would only be required for a month. Besides, winter was coming. Clearly they did not understand their own best interest. Clearly they did not see how Pottinger's plan – of eliminating or displacing the Xhosa – was their best chance of a settled future.

What foresight he was showing, to find a solution in shifting whole peoples to a separate and distant location. It was a lead subsequently followed by generations of officials.

The whole problem lay in the failure of the native peoples to understand how they were to be subject to the Queen; to understand that the military were not there to fire upon them and take back stolen cattle but were there to protect them. From whom? – from those who had so far failed to see reason, or the light, or the blessings of being a subject people. Those were Henry's instructions, that they must be made to accept their subordinate status.[10]

But like the amirs and the Chinese traders, the Bantu chiefs persisted in thinking only of their own interest. A leading Xhosa chief, Sandile, was asked to return 14 stolen goats found in one of his kraals, pay a fine of three head of cattle, and surrender the thief. Sandile confiscated the thief's property for himself, and did not return all the goats. Sir Henry would not permit such impudence. Sandile should be arrested, but the squadron sent to carry out this task found themselves opposed by close to a thousand warriors, and thought it more valorous to retire from the field.

Sir Henry was determined to make an unmistakable statement of force. He declared Sandile a rebel and once more he called up the burghers. Only 200 answered that call, even though he held out to them the offer of loot, the old East India Company practice – they could have all the cattle they could seize. Unhappily, and it was none of Sir Henry's doing, at exactly this time there were one or two episodes of a citizen wagon driver who had been flogged by the army for not going out to get firewood, and who had laid a charge of assault on the officer who had ordered the punishment. The court found that under martial law the officer was justified. That did not fill the burghers with enthusiasm.

As massive a force as could be contrived – some 2000 troops, both regular and irregular – marched out, or rode out, to Sandile's territory; but as previously, the tribesmen just kept melting away, or stayed hidden in among the crags and thickets. The British troops could do very little other than burn huts and keep riding about on patrol, preventing the natives from returning to their old way of life, preventing their return to their homelands. After some weeks of this incessant harassment, Sandile and his counsellors, tired of living out in the bush, surrendered. And in turn, one by one the other chiefs submitted to the British.

The Governor was obliged to let Sir George thrash around with all this. He, Sir Henry, was not to command the Queen's forces. So he resorted to an alternative manoeuvre: he formed a police force from the Khoikhoi population, the Hottentots. That was not welcomed by the farmers and burghers, however, who were apprehensive about allowing them any authority whatsoever, and were most unhappy about allowing them arms. Until relatively recently, they had been slave labour on the farms. And the settlers suspected they were secretly assisting the Xhosa.

As commissioner, it was for Pottinger to establish the terms on which the Xhosa would be offered peace; and by mid-December every chieftain in the projected territory of British sovereignty had come to terms with the new dispensation.[11]

But Sir Henry was not to savour the moment for long. He was to be transferred to Madras, back to the ministrations of the East India Company, and his successor had already landed in Cape Town – replacing him from 1 December, though the seals of office were not handed over (just outside Grahamstown) until 16 December. He had maintained much the same policy of inflexibility, and with much the same success as in India and in China, for which he was deservedly honoured. His own people back home knew his worth. Never mind that in the years that followed the subject peoples felt resentment.

He was off to India, in the same steamer that had brought the new governor from there. Sir George was to accompany him, which must have made the courtesies of travel somewhat stiff. And his secretary, Woosnan, was to accompany him too. An old India hand, Woosnan would be useful, as well as used to Sir Henry's ways. Also, he was doubtless privy to some aspects of Henry's private life. Better to keep him close to hand.

Before he left, Sir Henry had one last salvo to fire. Exasperated by muddle and inefficiency and incompetence, as he saw it, he had written his detailed criticisms back to London; and he took it upon himself to have the accompaniments to his dispatch published separately and after he left the Cape. It would show the colony just what needed attention.

Was ever such a great man so misunderstood? Here he was, being helpful, contributing to the common good, yet it was read as one tremendous flood of criticism. It was considered as weasel-like – or mongoose if you prefer – that his observations were not released until after he had left. And he had concentrated his remarks so that there should be only sensible analysis and no airy-fairy sweetening, but that was then read as unrelenting criticism. The bureaucracy was stunned that he had violated regulations in publishing at all. They failed to appreciate the public-mindedness of his action in doing so.

Was he eccentric in this? Not at all, just pragmatic. That is the disadvantage of greatness. It takes time for the rest of us to understand the grounds on which extraordinary actions are taken, and then to appreciate the integrity of it all.

He did not conceal his distaste for the British merchants with their extensive corruption and idleness, and the burgher militia was a riff-raff enamoured of their bogus military titles.

The newspapers were noisy in riposte. The *Cape Frontier Times* thought his remarks were defamatory: how long was 'this callous, unprincipled libeller to bask like a crocodile in the favour of Her Majesty's Government?'[12] Such a hostile response might be seen, *au contraire*, as confirming his estimation of the community he had just left behind. Clearly it was no acknowledgement of an habitual smile and thick skin.

But in a deeper sense, even the ingrates had to acknowledge, despite themselves, the grand narrative of Pottinger greatness. That basking crocodile, where does that come from if not upstream along the Nile, the antecedent wellspring of which has been acknowledged through the countless generations – countless in the sense of uncertainty about 31 or 32.

Pottinger did not leave a grateful colony behind him. There would be no presentations of silver plate this time. Nor, it seems, did he regretfully leave behind any distressed Mrs Morgan. Instead, he left a general feeling of ill will. Some years later, his incumbency was summarised in this way:

> He left this country without the esteem of a single colonist, though everyone acknowledged him to be a man of rare ability and great industry. No other governor of this colony ever lived in such open licentiousness as he. His amours would have been inexcusable in a young man, in one approaching his sixtieth year they were scandalous. In other respects a cold, calculating, sneering, unsympathetic demeanour prevented men of virtue from being attracted to him.[13]

That reads like the sour grapes of a much less vital man, envious of the accomplishments of a latter-day Mark Antony, or a Caesar who came and saw and conquered. The Pottinger accomplishment has to be recognised for what it was – and he, when would we see his like again? Or where?

VIII

FORTUNE'S WEAL

He who aspires to be a hero ... must drink brandy.

—JAMES BOSWELL, *The Life of Samuel Johnson*

HENRY ARRIVED IN Madras in early April 1848, and settled down for a standard six-year term. Everything had finally fallen into place – at least, in terms of his career. He had become a serial governor. His wife and children, however, preferred to live at a distance, whether in England or the Channel Islands or a hotel in Paris, wherever his good fortune would maintain them.

If Madras was not good enough for them, that was their missed opportunity. At one stage he sent for young Freddy to come out and be his aide-de-camp, but Lady Pottinger objected to that.[1]

Government Garden House, meaning a retreat from the site of official duties, was on a very large estate, all gleaming white and just adjacent to the grand Banqueting House. This, with its colonnaded terrace and rows and rows of columns like a Greek temple, was altogether on a more impressive scale than the somewhat grand but heavy residence originally designed by Edward Clive (son of the more famous Robert Clive), and enlarged and modified by each subsequent resident in turn. It shows. Sir Henry dabbled in that respect too, just like his predecessors. It had a grand new drive, and grand gates, and an iron fence; and a colourful mounted household guard, which managed its ceremonial manoeuvres with grand ostentation.

Unhappily, Madras is set on a vast arid plain and the grounds faithfully mirrored that setting. There was plenty of space to go galloping about, and Sir Henry rode down to the government offices every Tuesday morning, for a public breakfast and then to chair the Executive Council meeting.[2] Sir Henry was not one for walking anywhere if he could help it. That was far too commonplace – too pedestrian in point of fact.

One of his first acts was to write to the Court of Directors of the East India Company in London, to request approval for the formation of a museum, as proposed by the Madras Literary Society. It all seems to be a convergence from his past. The classical Greek temple of the Bombay Literary Society and its library, which supported Sir Henry's own researches when he wrote his book about Belochistan, corresponded to the great Hall just next door to his official residence, and now he was moving to institute a comparable cultural basis on this other side of India.

But lest we think that somewhat precious, it is to be noted that at the same time Sir Henry was elected unopposed to become the first president of the Madras Cricket Club, figuratively to open the batting. Such activity was the exclusive preserve of expatriate Englishmen, a second MCC. What masterly strategy. There was no surer way to excite the interest of local residents in the game.

Just out of town was a bay where the British officials had established a little community to escape the summer heat, along the backwaters at Ennore. Edward Clive had built himself a cottage there; now Sir Henry took over the tenancy, almost as a matter of course. That was more likely for gin and tonics than for yachting, though his uncle in Belfast, troublesome Thomas, had been handy with both. For it began to be whispered of Sir Henry that he had taken to drink. It must have been all that tippling with Kiying, all for the sake of the British Empire.

Another benefit of his new posting was that Madras featured a disproportionate number of unattached females,[3] which in itself was enough to spice up social encounters. After all, this is where Richard Wellesley had found the climate terribly exciting, the justification for all his amours. These were Sir Henry's last years in service, and it was time for him to enjoy the rewards of it. If not now, then when?

Which is not to imply that he was avoiding his responsibilities. Far from it. He dug sods to inaugurate a stretch of railway line, he created a body called 'the University board', he was all in favour of founding whatever needed to be founded, and was just as careful as ever about whatever needed to be funded – his expertise in this respect might well have found its origin in the family business in Belfast. And he did the bidding of the Court of Directors. It was they who required him to cancel a trial of growing cotton from American seed. Reports at the time were stunned at how abruptly the decision was made, and unfairly blamed Sir Henry for it. He, however, knew who his masters were. He would not be browbeaten by noisy public opinion. That was never his way. That was never the Pottinger way either.

He signed documents where he had to sign, he sent off troops as requested from time to time, to help keep the increasingly restless natives in line, he was horrified at the mishmash of Chillianwallah, as his old colleague General Gough attempted to bring the second Anglo-Sikh war to something like a successful conclusion. All the cavalry charges notwithstanding, Pottinger had no wish to join in the blood and glory. Instead, he kept a close eye on expenditure in the commissariat. He did as he was asked and he did what was expected of him. But not a lot more than that, and not always as promptly as he might have once upon a time. In fact, he was becoming increasingly resistant to change. For him, the old ways, the tried ways, recommended themselves.

He would not be taken for granted; and when the Governor-General expostulated with Sir Henry over delays in supplying needed troops, he made it clear that he had not been consulted on matters of how the military operations were to be conducted, and reminded the Governor-General that he had considerable experience in planning such manoeuvres. His irritability had not moderated at all.

Towards the end of 1851, the Queen signed a warrant for him to hold the rank of lieutenant-general in the regular army. That was sweet recognition, even though it came late in his career. He had another year or two to relish it before his time was up in Madras, to maintain his stance as the Queen's man more than a prestigious officer of John Company. But he was nearing 65, and he had spent long periods of his life in uncomfortable conditions. Those had taken their toll.[4] So too had his damnable gout.

His incumbency ended 24 April 1854. Unhappily, his departure was briefly delayed because his intended replacement died, more or less at the moment of learning the news. There he was, mortified – both of them were, in fact, but in different ways. An acting governor was scratched up and Henry returned to England a little later than he had anticipated, broken in health and needing to rest and mend.

We do not suggest that is a euphemism. We observe though that the expression has been used in such a way on other occasions.

He returned to reacquaint himself with a changed family. His wife had enjoyed her years of travelling about to various modish resorts and destinations. Their daughter, Henrietta, had married at the end of October 1850, as soon as she had turned 21; Sir Henry had missed both events. He had now a son-in-law to meet and to become acquainted with, a man called Stephens, though it appears there had been some correspondence while Henry was in Madras – at the very least, proper form would have demanded that Stephens request for his daughter's hand (in which case the fact of Henrietta having attained her majority is of interest) and respond to some questions about financial security – Stephens had recently graduated from Oxford – and about a likely dowry.

With Henrietta now a young married woman, Lady Susanna required an escort from time to time, and that appears to be why Frederick was extracted from Eton. He was fond of the racing track and he had gradually acquired an interest likewise in green baize tables; but he could be charming as required, when required, by his mother.

In 1850, at the time of his sister's wedding, Frederick followed his father into a world of uniforms and military parades and formal dinners and travel. He bought a commission in the Grenadier Guards. Or perhaps Henry provided the wherewithal and the connections. This was a prestigious regiment, and commissions came at a price. It was the most senior of the guards division, infantry not cavalry, which might strike us as odd, given Frederick's emerging disposition; but then we need to consider that he may well have understood himself better than we can. Henry, we recall, had made the same early choice.

Freddy was a lieutenant, just as his father had started out in the Bombay days. A famous regiment, its scarlet jackets and bearskins as eye-catching then as now,[5] no soldier was less than six feet two inches tall. They had a well-earned reputation among the ladies; they boasted military accomplishments too. They were well able to rival Napoleon's famed Imperial Guard at Waterloo, and defeated them. All big men, their expertise was in heavy fighting at close quarters. Which gives us some sense of what Freddy was growing into. With his masses of curling black hair and his large expressive eyes, he would have looked very presentable in any society matron's drawing room, and his mother must have been proud to make an entrance leaning on his arm.

This has all the makings of a chapter from *Vanity Fair*.

Frederick was just as susceptible as his fellows to the near-swooning attentions of any young miss, and he began to develop something of a reputation. He too had reached his majority in his father's absence. He had a figure to keep, and that meant womanising and quite possibly a little discreet whoring, and rather more card playing and long evenings at the roulette table – whether in London or, as later, in Paris, where his mother liked to put up at a favourite hotel. Dashing and handsome, Freddy lived rather fast. He was not one to back down from any gambling challenge, whether the cut of the cards or the tumble of dice, or the bookies' odds at a racecourse. He was extravagant, he was a diehard punter. Tailor-made for Australia, when the time came. Though having to borrow from his mother to settle some of his debts was not altogether good form.

When Britain sent off its troops to the Crimea in 1852, Freddy's regiment did not travel with them. Either by nimble-footedness or pure good luck, he stayed back at the Wellington Barracks, adjacent to the Palace, and helped to keep the home fires burning. His companions in arms covered themselves in glory – four of the Grenadiers in the 3rd regiment were awarded the Victoria Cross. Frederick though was not fastidious about honours. If honours were to be bestowed upon him, he would accept them graciously enough, but he was not one to hunt for them. He had his hands full, and his pockets otherwise, closer to Knightsbridge. He did however benefit in one particular from staying behind, for when his commanding officer, the Duke of Wellington died (September 1852), he was in the guard of honour at St Paul's Cathedral.[6]

And that in little is what awaited Sir Henry on his return to London in June 1854. This was quite different from the triumphal return 10 years earlier. His son and heir had to be taken into hand at once. There were debts to settle, affairs to tidy over, and the house at Eaton Place to be put back to sorts – it had been leased out while Sir Henry was on duty overseas, which detail contributes its own small understanding to the family's domestic arrangements.

Clearly Henry had been taking prudent steps for the duration. In his absence he had little need for such a grand address. His wife had been provided with the wherewithal to enjoy herself.

Now what to do about Freddy? His son had missed his chance for honours on the battlefield – that was a sad misjudgement, or an unfortunate outcome. And he had hardly been covering himself with glory at home. At the end of that first month, it was gazetted that Frederick was handing in his resignation and selling his commission (27 June 1854); either Henry had demanded that, or the army had, but either way Freddy was being retrieved before he was disgraced.

Henry felt this matter very deeply. Even before the notice had been gazetted, he wrote to his son-in-law Stephens not from Eaton Place but from Norwich, in which he refers to 'unpleasant matters' and hopes to have the benefit of distancing himself a little from them, and if not then to sell up his house. He proposed he might put his affairs in order to 'go back to India, where I shall keep aloof from all such annoyances and miseries'.[7] Whatever we might choose to understand by Henry's concern with his health, it did not mend easily; and he did not like the brouhaha in which he found himself entangled. He shuttled between Eaton Place and Norfolk and, curiously,

Turnham Green near Hammersmith, not all that far away – a distance which might be measured in terms of distaste.

Once again, the explanation seems to rest with young Frederick. On 23 May 1855, Freddy laid a bet at the Epsom Derby. He wagered £10,000 on Lord of the Isles to win – in modern terms that is heading up towards a big slice of a million dollars. He must have been confident. He knew horses. And that was a fine Irish-sounding name if ever there was one. To be sure.

The luck, the rub of the green, was not with him. His horse came in third, at 7/4 and just a whisker or whatever it is that horses have behind the second-place getter, but a rather definitive two lengths behind the winner. That would become the hallmark of Freddy's subsequent career: close, yet in the end not close enough.

This must be when his father disowned him. For Henry, it was the last straw. Damned if he was going to bail out the young wastrel. Lady Susanna was somewhat fonder of her boy, though, and sold her diamonds. Which reveals a significant difference in parental attachment.

In July of 1855 Henry wrote his last will and testament and then almost immediately set out for Malta, for a change of scenery, to escape the coming British winter, and to remove himself from his family.

His daughter Henrietta and his second son Harry both attempted a reconciliation with him. Henrietta in particular resolved never to leave her father again (though she was no more attracted than was her mother to the prospect of spending years in India, should it come to that). They were instrumental in moderating Henry's anger. In December he wrote a codicil to his will, and a second one in January, both of these in Valletta, the capital of Malta, with the upshot that, first, Frederick – who after all would inherit his title – should be his executor and then, on second thoughts, that maybe there should be more than a few others involved, just to keep an eye on things, even though Frederick was reconciled with him more or less on his deathbed.

Sir Henry was not reconciled to his final lot in life, though:

> Before Pottinger died, in Malta in 1856, he was visited by Lord Glanville, the Leader of the House of Lords, who reported that he had 'just seen Sir H. Pottinger living in retirement and bearing in addition to a load of infirmities, the most painful burden of soreness and mortification at the neglect of his services'.[8]

He died in March 1856, aged sixty-six, and was buried there. As is all but inevitable – think of Rome – his grave has been ravaged by time, war, neglect and vandalism, a kind of affirmation of his greatness because that leaves his accomplishments to speak for themselves. They did not need to be chiselled in obscure Latin verse on a slab of marble. Alfred the Great fared no better.

Henry's title fell to Frederick, whose first responsibility was to see that his father's will was properly carried out. On 14 February 1857, the *Illustrated London News* carried a brief notice that Sir Henry's estate was sworn at £70,000. Freddy was left to finalise matters because the additional executors all, in the quaint terminology of the law, 'renounced', as though they had lost confidence in the matter. Another gentleman was responsible for whatever needed sorting out in Madras.

Freddy was exemplary, he rose to the occasion. He was heir to everything, but he ensured that:

> The service of plate presented to him [Sir Henry] by the merchants of Malta, the silver salver by the inhabitants of London, Manchester, and Liverpool, the gold armlet by his Excellency Keying, on his negotiating the Treaty of Nankin, and the clock and two vases by the ladies of Madras, [were] to be held as heirlooms with the baronetcy, and the possession of the mansion in Eaton-place.[9]

It is a wickedness to blur this detail, as some have done, into a charge that Freddy sold off the family silver; that may have happened later but not at this juncture. He had arranged that his mother should continue to reside in her home, and possibly his brother too, for the time being. This is the side of Freddy that we should esteem.

And being careful as his father had been careful, Freddy declined to pay legacy duty, arguing that his father had been domiciled in India, not England, and was in fact on his way to India when he died in Malta. The Court of Exchequer had a fine old time of that, for it took another five years to settle the matter. Frederick's case was based on affidavits from various of the family, who all affirmed that Sir Henry couldn't wait to get away from everything and back to India – notwithstanding his own declaration in his will that he resided in Eaton Place. That would not discourage Sir Frederick. He knew better. He knew what his father intended, and he knew he would prefer not to pay the duty. He could be resolute when he wanted. And he was now head of the family with more than enough of a fortune near his fingertips. And plenty of leisure in which to spend it.

Later that year, at the height of summer, when anybody who was anybody had departed to somebody else's country house or to the Continent, Frederick was taken to court for non-payment of a bill. Well, something a bit more sensational, and embarrassing, than that. At dinner on a Saturday evening at the Great Western Royal Hotel, the grand new establishment near Paddington Station, he was arrested on suspicion that he might be trying to flee the country. As if a Pottinger would stoop to any such low behaviour.

This took place in April, the month after the will was proven and Frederick was at last master of his own fate. At issue was a bill for £84 – something like £2500 today – to a housing agent and furniture dealer, or maybe an upholsterer. Given Freddy's wealth, that should not have been a problem; but it was a problem as far as Sir Frederick was concerned. He thought the amount was exorbitant. He had been presented with a bill for half that and was prepared to hand over a £20 note on the spot. Cash in hand, literally. He was convinced that the grasping merchant classes were trying to exploit him, and that was enough to get his very Pottingeresque dander up. What we see in this is that he had quite properly moved away from his own family's Belfast beginnings. Greatness will out.

The awkwardness was that he had accepted responsibility for expenses incurred by the tenant there, at Cambridge Place, Pimlico. And the tenant was a young Miss Perry, originally of Stanley Road, which was a less salubrious suburb and somewhat out of the way of Sir Frederick, who was now her 'protector'. He paid her bills, he paid her maintenance, he paid off some of her debts. This was all to emerge in August, when the action went to trial, for Sir Frederick denied liability.

At the trial proper, the judge had offered Sir Frederick the arrangement of a special jury, given his, Sir Frederick's, status. But he had a proper sense of honour, he would not dodge the public eye. He had nothing to conceal. As the narrative story unfolded bit by bit, it does no credit to those who attended that there were frequent instances of tittering. Sir Frederick had first met Miss Perry at a dinner, attended by two or three other friends, one among whom was a colonel rather less affluent than our hero, and who could not well sustain the expense of maintaining his role as Miss Perry's protector. This too had happened in April. Whether that was the occasion of the dinner at the Great Western Royal Hotel is not clear. The learned counsel neglected his opportunity to press the matter.

Miss Perry and some of her furniture were moved into the newly leased premises, the furniture cleaned, a piano and other articles provided; and given she was regularly paying down a debt for jewellery, Freddy paid off what was owing on that. These are all patently the measured actions of a generous and charitable gentleman, and it does Sir Frederick particular credit. Less clear is why in the first instance he drew up the lease for the Pimlico premises in the name of John Perry, of Bath. He seemed to think that this would allow him to avoid jury duty, whereas one might have thought his proper title would have protected him rather more. Whoever heard of a knight of the realm sitting on a jury?

Miss Perry, it turns out, could neither read nor write. In this, she was no rival to Becky Sharpe. But she did have an eye for expensive jewellery. According to some witnesses, on occasion she allowed herself to be addressed as Mrs Pottinger (in which case the John Perry alias did not carry much weight); sometimes, as Lady Pottinger, though Freddy denied that; and the servants addressed her as 'My Lady', which information provoked a laugh in the gallery.

Witnesses – servants, the cook – testified that Sir Frederick would sometimes stay the night there and take breakfast the next morning. And further to the merriment in court, and in the press, Sir Frederick would not allow Miss Perry to receive any visitors other than himself and was heard to have said that if he ever found anyone else in the house he would kick them out. The cook declined to say whether other gentlemen than Sir Frederick used to visit.[10]

Justice was done, and seen to be done. Sir Frederick was able to affirm that he was ignorant of all this business, and the court believed him. He never ordered a stick of furniture – it must have been that fellow Perry, of whom he knew nothing. The verdict was in his favour; but the hearing itself, and the unsavoury reporting by the press meant that it was politic to disappear for a while and lie low, in Cadiz, until the City had had its fill and looked to new sources of titillation.

On his return, he resumed his former ways, and rattled through his patrimony in fine style. He was no niggardly punter, as we saw when he placed the equivalent of 10 per cent of his inheritance on the disappointing Lord of the Isles. What speedier way of recouping his loss than by placing sizeable bets here, there and everywhere? Debt collectors began circling again, he resorted to selling off more of the family silver, for example, the silver plate presented to Sir Henry in Liverpool, and a huge candelabra from the Bombay merchants.[11] It was all too much for the family, including his doting mother. Quite simply, they could not afford him. And he could not afford Miss Perry either.

In March 1859, he took passage from Liverpool on the *British Trident*, a steam ship bound for Melbourne. Apparently he financed his passage from his winnings on a race.[12] The intention was to revive his fortunes on the Victorian goldfields. But he was a Pottinger after all; and digging for gold would of course have led him back to grubbing in the soil. Which is not exactly what he had had in mind for himself.

IX

A TOUCH OF ENGLISH

To be great is to be misunderstood.

—RALPH WALDO EMERSON, *Self-reliance*

WHEN THE *BRITISH Trident* berthed in Melbourne on 8 June 1859, there was no Sir Frederick Pottinger aboard. Listed at the top of the ship's manifest though, in the first-class cabins, was a Mr F.W. Parker. Freddy was travelling incognito. Wisely, he had held on to his initials – it would have been a pity to jettison all that monogrammed luggage.

Possibly because he had stepped aside from his own proper self, the fates were blindsided. For he arrived at the mouth of yet another river, coming (as it might be seen) towards the end of the vital currency of the Pottingers. Here was no delta, as prescribed by the overriding metaphor of that estimable family's lineage. The Yarra was baffled by a rocky cascade at what should have been its mouth. It did not spread out its richness into an intricate network of estuarine waterways, such as we have learned to expect. It did not ramify. The signs were not propitious.

Melbourne's winters are not highly regarded; and furthermore, Freddy had left his run to the goldfields somewhat late. The best of the pickings had already been, well, picked; the best of the diggings had been dug over. Fossickers had been through the mullock heaps time and again, and with little enough to show for their efforts.

On the fields he would have been forced to mingle with the great unwashed, a rough and ready lot from all over the world. This was the worst time of the year, cold, wet and muddy. Within a matter of months, he made the best of a bad job and abandoned that foray into the field of pipeclay dreams. He took passage on the *City of Sydney* via Twofold Bay and arrived in Sydney on 4 March, plain Mr Pottinger this time, though still a cabin passenger. Unnervingly, a Lieutenant Perry was aboard, and perhaps that coincidence encouraged him to play a straight bat.

And here we should reflect a little. Sir Frederick – Freddy for now, in his eclipse – had not behaved as well as we would want from such an exemplar. Colourful, lively, a good friend to his dining companions, generous in offering his protection to a young woman in need of such assistance as he had offered, we have to confess there is for us some modicum of concern about the family silver. No doubt Freddy regretted that. No doubt he regretted having to leave London. No doubt he regretted having placed a bet on Lord of the Isles, though beyond question that useless bag of bones should have won.

He had more than enough time to think about all of this on the long voyage out to the far side of the world. And we can understand what must have happened if we remember how another lively young rakehell, Prince Hal, transformed himself into the very model of greatness, when 'Consideration like an angel came,/ And whipp'd the offending Adam out of him'.[1] Destiny moves as it must in its own incontrovertible way.

Freddy was resolved to make a new man of himself here, in what a lesser being would regard as exile; but with a new heaven and a new earth he could start over once more. He had done his time, his 40 days and 40 nights and more in the wilderness, and he had come to see the error of his ways, as well as the inconvenience of disgrace. Besides, digging for gold was always a chancy business. Less exhausting by far to escort discovered gold from the diggings to the banks, to become a trooper – a mounted trooper. In this way we find him setting out for the southern districts, to attach himself to the New South Wales police force, and to the gold escort there.

It was like Alfred starting over again with a fresh batch of scones.

Freddy's assigned duties had him monitoring the new goldfields between Gundagai and Bathurst. He must have set off down that way quite quickly once he had made his decision, for he left behind three letters at the General Post Office in Sydney, each addressed to him under his real name but not apparently with his title.[2] His superior officer was based at Bathurst, and no doubt to begin with he would have had to report there, to be schooled in his various responsibilities. Even so, he spent enough time in Gundagai to make the acquaintance of Mrs Fry, hostess at the recently opened Fry's Hotel, the newest hotel in town.

Regrettably Mrs Fry lacked breeding. Large-hearted as he ever was, Freddy was prepared to overlook that unfortunate deficiency and allow her the benefit of his friendship whenever he was in town. In this he showed much the same generosity that had impelled him in that unfortunate interlude with Miss Perry in London. The ways of the great are truly remarkable, if we would only study them. Here though, we have to make an allowance. Having been sent out into the world on his own, Freddy was in need of friendship wherever he could find it.

When he wasn't politely attending to the friendly accommodation of his hostess, or braving the wilds galloping alongside a carriage loaded with gold, he had opportunity to write up his journal, in which he could give rein to his tender side, reviewing his life – heavens, he was already 30! – and transcribing some of the poems he had been moved to write by or for Miss Perry, among others.[3] It is a romantic image, the young man, something of a troubadour in the vast unknown of Australia, moist-eyed if not actually crying in the wilderness.

Now that he had a responsible public role, it was more acceptable for him to grow his beard instead of his hair, in the fashion of his Grenadier companions who had gone off to the Crimea; and possibly, looking much the same as the diggers among whom he had toiled on the Victorian goldfields. In his new role he lived close to the frontier, among wild young fellows who were all impatient to be bearded in like fashion, a bushy beard for preference. That was the fashion too of the radical young bohemians in Europe. Though come to think of it, Freddy's own father and his cousin Eldred had both grown a significant beard as part of their Middle Eastern disguise.

Freddy no longer appeared a poetical youth; he looked more severe, he looked like someone who could deal with miscreants, and certainly someone who could look after himself.

Here, in the rough and tumble backblocks, it was appropriate for him to fit in with his new surroundings, to show himself to be a man. And it was now that he began to learn the ways of the bush, the distances of the different stages that had to be covered, how to find water, where to make camp – the rudiments of bushcraft. There was no question that he could ride, and ride well; but this form of riding was more challenging than that of his Irish relations galloping out and about over the soft green fields of Belfast.

Whether through the sympathetic ministrations of Mrs Fry or just the restorative action of time itself, Freddy was beginning to feel more and more like his former self. Indeed, he was starting to champ at the bit. He could feel the urge to make a name for himself – or rather, to present his name to the world, or that part of it which mattered. Why, even Mrs Fry did not know the truth about him; though his superiority – his charm, his elegant manners, his breeding, his very class – must have been attractively evident to her.

He considered the matter and hit on a cunning stratagem. He wrote a letter addressed to himself, his *proper* self, care of his superior, Captain Battye in Bathurst. In due course an advertisement appeared in the *Bathurst Free Press* that Captain Battye had 'received a letter addressed to Sir Fred. Pottinger, Bart, Mounted Police, Bathurst; and anyone able to give information regarding the said Sir Frederick Pottinger would oblige by communicating with Captain Battye, Bathurst'.[4]

This was an ingenious move. Now the whole colony would know who was in their midst. Captain Battye, who was never one for keeping up with the paperwork, must have been astonished to learn that he had a baronet in his employ. And while Freddy waited in the wings, that remarkable item of information was sent speeding towards Sydney, for normally such a personage would have introduced himself to Government House. There had been no advance notice of his arrival in the colony. Why, this Sir Frederick may very well have been the governor's social equal. And if he were serving in the mounted police, how was this not known by those in the force? Was he being treated with the courtesy due to his title? Why had he been seeking virtual anonymity? It all had to be looked into forthwith.

Freddy's letter was sent to Bathurst in early May, less than a month after his arrival in Sydney. Six months later, by the beginning of November, a vacancy had been found for him to fill, the role of Clerk of Petty Sessions at Dubbo. That had been a topic of discussion by the Governor and the Executive Council, and then publicly gazetted.

News of the appointment was copied and repeated throughout the colony, indeed in the adjacent colonies too. And distressing as it is to reveal this, that news was not always received in the press with the respect that might have been anticipated. Some (for example, the *Armidale Express*) unkindly commented that the announcement had caused 'some amusement'. Others noted that this put a titled personage in a subordinate position. Not only Mrs Fry was displaying a want of breeding.

In a matter of weeks Sir Frederick's brief was expanded, to include serving as Registrar of Births, Deaths and Marriages in Dubbo, in place of a deceased predecessor (whose own record he would have to write up). His worth was at least appreciated by those whose opinions mattered. His salary, though – quite a different matter – was no more than £50 per annum.

His superiors saw he performed his duties faithfully and regularly, although the workplace conditions left something to be desired:

> The place used for a courthouse is one of those miserable log huts, where the rain in any quantity makes its way through the shingles on to the vouchers; and as to the gaol, why anyone can put small things through the interstices of the logs or slabs. The only wonder is how the gaoler contrives to keep his confines so safely.[5]

Soon he was made responsible for assessing the census results in Dubbo; and his expertise with horses was so readily apparent that he was invited to act as judge at an upcoming race meeting at Dubbo. The original shallow mirth at his expense had ceased; he was being acknowledged for what he really was, what should have been evident from the outset, a leader in the community.

By astonishing chance, his appointment in Dubbo almost brought about another of those extraordinary events that mark the trajectory of our great figures. For John Jardine, one of the Jardines of Spedlins Tower, uncle of the Jardines of Hong Kong, had migrated to Australia some 20 years earlier and had in that time become the Police Commissioner in Wellington, near Dubbo, close enough by bush standards to have been a professional acquaintance. Only Freddy, being Freddy, had left his run a bit late. By the time he arrived, the Jardines lived in Rockhampton, where the two sons had made a name for themselves by setting out with a sizeable mob of sheep and cattle and droving them – or a fair number of them – through the most punishing distances and difficult terrain all the way to the top end of Cape York.

If matters had been otherwise, an encounter could have happened. In the great scheme of things that was another near miss, much like his horse coming a close third at Epsom.

The Jardine boys' extraordinary trek took them right through Queensland, where Freddy's school chum from Eton days, Robert Herbert, had just become the first premier of that new colony. It never ceases to amaze how markedly significant personages and events swirl about the lives of the great and hint at a hitherto unidentified pattern. In this case we have a point of intersection, not of convergence, but it is nevertheless another of the curious narratives that together make up our colonial history.[6]

In the Pottinger case, it is a pattern of what nearly was, of what might have been.

Before the year was out, Sir Frederick was gazetted to be Assistant Superintendent of the Southern Patrol and Gold Escort in Dubbo; it was no doubt a momentary lapse on his part that he forgot to resign from his previous role as Registrar until nearly a fortnight after taking up his new role. At the beginning of November, just one year after his appointment, he was moved to fill a vacancy at Burrangong, right on the edge of the latest goldfield and just five or six miles from Lambing Flat – where already the behaviour of diggers towards the numbers of Chinese was becoming unpleasant, and the first intimations of riot was surfacing. Sir Frederick's 'camp' was a ready reserve of additional troopers, should need arise. Or rather, when the need arose. He led the night patrols when, for example, the 'Donegalers' began celebrating the New Year in a somewhat unruly and disruptive manner.

All this highly creditable activity is exactly what the authorities had expected from him. He was made a magistrate too, a Commissioner of the Peace. No wonder he ceased to write his journal. He simply had not the time. In any case he was now based at a distance from Mrs Fry. His thoughts were no longer languid reminiscences but were all concentrated on assembling information to counter the rising number of offences taking place along the roads and in hotels and bush shanties – and more worrying than that other major activity in the district, the theft of horses. Some of those horses were of very good stock indeed. He knew: he himself had bought a thoroughbred, confusingly named Arabian Star. Arabian horses are not thoroughbreds.

Sir Frederick did not seem to see the difficulty there. It was a better name than his father's Bandicoot.

That raises a different question, however, and the answer to it is uncertain. Sir Frederick's rate of pay was not extraordinary, even if the man was. He had exhausted his patrimony in England, some millions of dollars in terms of modern values. He had been fortunate in winning enough money on a bet to pay for his first-class passage to Melbourne, and then to Sydney. He had appeared to some advantage at a ball at Burrangong, showing the locals how they used to do it at Knightsbridge. And now he had bought a rather fine horse, and stabled it, and that did not come cheap. It would be a good guess that his mother remained well disposed towards him, and made occasional – if not regular – remittances to him. We simply do not know, just as we know so little about his venerable ancestor, Alfred the Great.

But we do know some other matters, which emerged on the occasion of yet another court appearance. Or rather, several. How his family must have despaired at these occasions of self-inflicted publicity.

First – and we can see for ourselves how entirely blameless the young man was in what transpired – at some time in December 1861 he was approached by a highly irate woman, 'a fine big strapping Irish woman',[7] variously identified as the landlady, hostess, licensee and/or owner of a reasonably prominent hotel just outside Forbes and on the Lambing Flat road. This untamable shrew flounced into his office brandishing a horsewhip and shrilly demanded him to acknowledge that he had sent a letter to the Horse and Jockey Hotel, where it appears she had established herself. He was remarkably cool, even disdainful; she had to be restrained by an attendant sergeant. Given the great uproar she created, Freddy did what anyone in his circumstances would have done: he had her shut in a cell. And immediately after, took her to the police court.

The magistrate was not persuaded that the tone of the letter was offensive, and bound her over to keep the peace.[8]

The woman in question was never going to get satisfaction; she had no lawyer to speak for her, and Sir Frederick held all the cards.

Now various inferences can be deduced from this. He was no longer within Mrs Fry's sphere of influence – not that it is suggested that Elizabeth Coyle, for that was the woman's name, may have replaced Mrs Fry in every particular. But Miss Coyle's public house had a name that would have attracted young Sir Frederick's eye. We know from details of a fire two years later in a hotel for which she held the licence that she owned an expensive billiard table,[9] so it does not take a lot to work out the other attractions she, or the premises, had to offer.

Nobody at the time missed the comparison with the infamous Lola Montez flourishing her whip at an editor in Ballarat; and nobody missed the little frisson that accompanied that reference either.

Late on a Friday night just after this, Sir Frederick had ridden past the Horse and Jockey Hotel, where we might safely speculate he was no longer welcome, into Lambing Flat in the company of several others (identified subsequently as from the police camp at Burrangong) and at the billiard table there took on the local shark, who had been playing and winning all day. Sir Frederick had confidence in his own game; a bystander entered a bet with him, and Freddy lost his tenner. As was customary, the winner shouted champagne, maybe two dozen bottles, and everyone – nine or 10 people were said to be in the room – partook of his largesse.

Then he challenged Sir Frederick to play a further match against the local man, £15 to his (Freddy's) £10. Sir Frederick was not one to squib a challenge. We note that he had enough ready money about him to meet the wager. And he soon justified his self-confidence. He was a Pottinger after all, and he performed just as we would expect of him. Before long he took the lead, and then gradually extended that lead; and as the game went on the bystander, one Thomas Watt, began to grow edgy and to call out a commentary on the match and the players. At some stage Watt flung a glass tumbler at a dog under the table; he was decidedly no gentleman.

In fact, he was a butcher whose business was also in Burrangong, so he should have known who Sir Frederick was. As the evening wore on and Freddy approached the end of the game, Watt began to accuse Freddy's opponent of throwing the match, and his money – setting aside that this fellow had been playing all day and it was now approaching 3 am. We should not let a minor detail get in the way of Sir Frederick's skill. No doubt he too had worked a long day, if not necessarily at that kind of table; surely he would have been tired too. Indeed, given the reputation of the diggers in Lambing Flat, he had very probably had a hard week of it. But never underestimate the Pottingers. They stayed the course.

When Watt accused the pool-hall player of being a swindler and a shooler, with a coarsely colonial adjectival emphasis, Sir Frederick asked him whether he, Watt, meant that to refer to him. He was not asking for clarification of what a shooler was – he knew perfectly well it was a kind of johnny-come-lately who was on the take wherever he saw an opportunity. No, Sir Frederick was asking whether the aspersion of cheating was meant to apply to him. Yes, to both of you, said Watt, hinting that he suspected some understanding, some arrangement between the two of them, which itself would have been enough to offend Sir Frederick. After all, he was a recently appointed magistrate and an assistant superintendent of the police, as must have been evident if he were still in his uniform.

Sir Frederick was even more enraged by the slight upon his gentlemanly honour and the insolence about being a newcomer. Honour demanded satisfaction, so did antagonism. The nearest weapon to hand was already in his hand. Using both he swung the billiard cue and cracked Watt over the head with it, drawing blood, and a scuffle broke out as very often does on such occasions.

Butchers have to be strong, to lump about whole sides of beef. Watt thought he was more than Pottinger's equal in this respect at least. But Freddy, ex-Grenadier, was up for the fight.

We remark that he did not reverse the cue and use the thick end of it as a long truncheon. He was fighting as a nobleman, not as a policeman. Certainly not as a butcher.

The scuffle did not last long, but long enough for Watt to shed his vest and for Freddy to rip his shirt, and then for Freddy to hit Watt in the eye with the billiard cue – that makes us wince – and finally to smash Watt's head through a window pane. One witness, who must surely have been mistaken, thought that Sir Frederick seemed afraid of the butcher, and was using the cue to fend him off. That was when the other bystanders jumped down from the table where they had been taking refuge, and separated the two. Anything more might have turned seriously ugly.

It is to be hoped that none of these were diggers. Their boots would have done the baize no good.

Sir Frederick had barely a scratch on him, for this tussle occurred just a matter of weeks before he appeared to such advantage at the local ball. But then that is the inherent nature of superiority, to show itself to advantage.

Watt claimed damages against Sir Frederick of £200, coincidentally the value of Miss Perry's necklace. There were no public reports of the fracas, however, until the trial two months after it occurred. The court took into account that Watt had previous convictions. Some time back he had hit and then knifed an abusive employee, and was sent to Bathurst goal for it; lucky for him he did not on that occasion reach for his cleaver. For a separate offence he had been summoned to court for assault just three months previously and had been fined.

It was therefore only fair that judge and jury should also take into account Sir Henry's personal history, as far as it was known in New South Wales, as well as that of Watt. The jury took only a few minutes to decide for the plaintiff, and damages were awarded – of just one shilling.[10]

That, any reasonable person would think, should have settled the matter. But the press, the colonial press, found the opportunity for irreverence too good to resist. They disregarded the testimony that Sir Frederick had been 'cool, quiet and sober'; they were more interested in the rounds of champagne and the lateness of the hour, when any lawful public house would have been closed. What was a magistrate doing there at that hour? And what was that about being a Commissioner of the Peace?

Freddy's timing was just awful. Not only did his actions conflict with his recent appointment, and not only had he to appear before the very man who had sworn him in as a JP, but he was about to embarrass the government hugely. Unbeknown to him, the authorities were on the point of a wholesale reorganisation of the police department, on quasi-military lines.

Up to this time the police force had operated regionally, with local magistrates calling the shots, so to speak. Some of these were inept; graft, drunkenness and pomposity were not unknown either. A good many of the old force were ticket-of-leave men. The authorities wanted to improve the credibility of the force, and why not?

They proposed to centralise everything; which in turn meant that one-half of the police would attend to matters in Sydney, and quite right too, given most of the population resided there. But soon enough it became evident that large masses of population were rushing to wherever the latest gold discoveries were; and that was where most of the bushranging activity occurred, not in Sydney. Meaning that the early welcome with which the reforms were received turned to scorn for the 'new police', and the new arrangements.

With the goldrushes came a spate of robberies and assaults in the goldfield districts; and as larger and larger consignments of gold were sent on to the security of regional centres, so the likelihood of hold-ups increased. Which was why Sir Frederick and his ilk were now patrolling the roads. But to the public the police had long been considered incompetent, and indeed the loyalty of some of them was in question, not to mention their sobriety. Many of the more stalwart types abandoned the force for the diggings. Besides, troopers and foot police were under separate commands. What was needed was a central unifying command. Of course. The wonder is that this centralised control had not already occurred. And as that was like a military line of command, it would have resonated with Sir Frederick, indeed with the Pottingers at large.

What was really needed was a command that paid heed to what was happening in the regions. Well, experience shows that you don't always get everything right all at once.

On 1 March 1862, a few months after the billiard table incident and at the very time of the trial, a new Police Regulation Act was promulgated, in which Sir Frederick was appointed as an inspector and assigned to the Lachlan, as it was still being called, though its name change to Forbes was already in train. His former superior, Captain Battye, was appointed to Lambing Flat. With the announcement, much emphasis was laid upon the importance of cultivating a proper regard for the respectability and general character of the force, with the warning of removal should members of the force lapse from the requisite standards of behaviour.

Imagine the consternation of the Colonial Secretary then, when Sir Fredrick's culpability was established in Yass court, and when that verdict was published not only in the local newspaper, but also copied into papers right across the colony. For Sir Frederick had been especially selected – indeed, he headed the list of inspectors – for his activity and application in the field. He was just the sort of man they wanted. This news of his now-criminal assault in the billiard room was wholly unacceptable.

Three weeks later, on 25 March, the Colonial Secretary released a public censure of his star recruit. It was sent to all officers in the force; it was published in all the newspapers. In firm measured tones, the reproof spelled out that while Sir Frederick had discredited himself as a gentleman, he had also demeaned the standing of the police force. He had exactly contradicted the intended outcome of the new Police Act, he had offended against a directive that members of the police force were not to frequent public houses (the letter avoided drawing attention to the lateness of the hour) and he had compromised his fitness to perform his duties on the following day. Any of these grounds would have seen a lesser mortal dismissed.

Any and all of those criticisms would have stung Sir Frederick. But he was a man of mettle. He had been appointed to a role, and he would perform that role. Even if, as was inevitable because some mark of disapproval had also to be made, he was transferred forthwith to a more remote posting, but still in the approximate region.

Or we might reflect that he was now inserted right into the heart of the diggings, where there was widespread unrest about the Chinese and increasing instances of robbery, including highway robbery. If this was an intention to throw him into the middle of outlawry, he was just the man to rise to the challenge. If anyone could do what had to be done, that was Inspector Pottinger.

It would have been preferable if the fierce billiard saloon altercation had not taken place at all. Sir Frederick was a gentleman, he knew he was a gentleman, and the social debris that collected in billiard rooms should know that gentlemen are not crawlers. Now he had to earn back his superiors' trust, and possibly that of his men too, given that some of the witnesses on the occasion were from his camp at Burrangong.

He could not take a trick, or so it seems. Yet is that a character flaw? For we can look at the matter another way. The real point is that he had the fortitude to persevere despite this reversal. And persist he did. This was not stubborn bullheadedness. We have to concede the man was simply splendid.

It would be too much of course to expect the colonial press to be respectful about Sir Frederick's loss of face. The editorials were quick to point out the moral failings here. Not only was he setting a bad example, he had surrendered to his own weakness – billiards late into the night was bad enough, wagering on the outcome was worse[11] – but he was behaving just like the locals. How low could he sink?

To confirm Freddy's wretched sense of timing, all this open commentary came just in the wake of a breezily disrespectful published letter from an unusual correspondent, the bushranger Frank Gardiner.

For about a year, newspapers had been remarking on the increasing frequency with which Frank Gardiner and his gang had raided properties and robbing travellers along the road between Burrangong (where Sir Frederick had been stationed) and Forbes (where Sir Frederick was about to be stationed). Gardiner had taken to providing a review of his recent activities in the district and making cheap provocative remarks in passing about the Inspector, though the implication is that he did not know Sir Frederick well, or had not yet encountered him.

On 18 March, with mock facetiousness he referred to the tempting prospect of robbing a 'real live barrownight'; but equally he observed that as Pottinger had come to the road in question, he (Gardiner) should keep away.[12] That, of course, could have been deliberately misleading, designed to encourage travellers to relax their vigilance. As if Gardiner had not been provocative enough, he then remarked that Pottinger was more than a hundred miles away, looking in the wrong place, and that meant the road was in fact clear for Gardiner to do as he would. The man's cheek was intolerable. He referred to the Inspector as 'poor Pilgarlic', so drawing attention to Sir Frederick's receding hairline – and Freddy had only that week turned 31. What an affront! If Gardiner's intention was to goad Sir Frederick and win the support of the rural poor, then his insolence might very well work the trick.

And here we pause once more to marvel at how the lives of the inestimably great all contrive to forge a pattern. For just as we saw in contemplating the origin of the name Pottinger and its bizarre near-convergence with Jardine, so here is another substantial player contributing to the plot, so to speak – Frank Gardiner. From where did he conjure up that name? His real name was Christie, though he sometimes took his mother's name, Clark, as another alias. It is almost as though he intuitively knew what to call himself to take his place in this unlikely cast of characters, all descended, if we attend to their names, from dibblers.

But back to the public insolence of this newspaper puff – call it colonial cheek if you will – it is just possible these were not Gardiner's words at all. As reported, he seems to have an exceptional range of reference. Those who, learning that his nickname was 'Darkie', assume he had Aboriginal ancestry, might find its vocabulary and allusiveness difficult to accept, for if such were indeed the case one might presume that his opportunities to acquire such a range should have been somewhat limited.[13]

Just a few weeks after this, the *Sydney Morning Herald* copied a paragraph from the *Lachlan Miner*:

> Sir F. Pottinger slipped away the other evening in disguise, taking with him sundry aboriginals, who could 'smell the colour of the hair of any man', and a fair dose of mounted police noted for their bravery. As they left Forbes in the distance, the very man they had gone out to hunt down passed them, took their measure, and sauntered into the town of Forbes to enjoy himself, patronizing the Standard and the Exhibition, taking his quiet liquor, and studying 'ye manners and ye customs of ye Fubbites in ye Inspector's absence'.[14]

There are several points to make here. This is the first indication we have that Sir Frederick was now making use of blacktrackers – and these were to become very important when he went out into the field. Second, we have to consider whether it was altogether a wise strategy to empty the town of policemen and so leave it comfortably accessible by Gardiner. Whoever reported this event clearly identified his presence; but unfortunately, there was now no residual authority to whom it could be reported.

Doubtless, Sir Frederick had his own concealed reasons, not least of which would have been his need for as massive a force as he could gather to capture the ever-elusive bushranger.

Thirdly, Sir Frederick was in disguise. We have no clear information about whether the troopers were also in disguise. What we should know was that it was no longer insisted that the police should go out into the countryside in full uniform – that was too much of an advantage for their quarry. As though it might not occur to any skulking bushrangers that a massive armed party represented anything out of the ordinary.

But above all, we have to observe what happened on the road out of town. Sir Frederick and his troopers failed to recognise Frank Gardiner. Neither did the blacktrackers, who must have been concentrating on hair colour to the exclusion of all other detail. Or possibly because his hair smelled acceptable to them, they let him pass without comment. Whereas Gardiner is reported to have taken their measure as he trotted by. Whatever was Freddy looking at, if not every single rider he encountered? Of course, we have only the word of the reporter, who was not even there. In fact, the only witness to this incident would have been Gardiner himself – and we have to allow that he had a vested interest.

Or maybe this is a succinct example of how Sir Frederick came to public attention. For Freddy simply hadn't noticed anything untoward, he simply didn't see it.

While taking his ease in Forbes, Gardiner placed an advertisement for half a dozen apprentices, who must each provide themselves with a bowie knife, a revolver, a pair of corduroys, and jack boots. References would be required. The advertisement appeared adjacent to the notice about Sir Frederick slipping away incognito; and it appeared, as did that notice, in the *Lachlan Miner*.[15] The notice was of course copied by other papers too as a good joke.

A pity about that, because Sir Frederick was not gifted with a sense of humour.

X

THE ILL-TEMPERED CAVALIER

I have seen the moment of my greatness flicker.

—T.S. ELIOT, *The love song of J. Alfred Prufrock*

BILLY DARGAN, A Wiradjuri man, was one of those Aboriginals, though whether in disguise or still awaiting his uniform has not been made known to us. Others were Johnny the Dealer,[1] and Black Pilot, and Charley Edwards (possibly also known as 'Prince Charlie'[2]). They were all expert trackers, Billy in particular,[3] again and again making out the trail of bushrangers even while riding at a gallop. Freddy couldn't. How that must have stuck in the Pottinger craw, virtually conceding the leadership of his party in the field to a subordinate and an inferior. His father had the same low estimate of lesser peoples, those unfortunate enough not to have been born British; and preferably, British to the bootstraps.

For the best part of a fortnight Freddy and his troopers, and his trackers, scoured the countryside. In their absence, while they were out and about on their business, seven prisoners escaped from the Forbes lock-up – unhappily for Sir Frederick, not so for the escapees. That did not improve his record, nor his temper. And to add insult to injury, the very man he was looking for bailed up a pair of drays just outside Forbes and relieved them of their payload of gin and tobacco, among other commodities. Gardiner was identified by the owner of those two rigs and reported to whomever had been left behind at the police station; and so was another famous figure, or one about to become famous, Ben Hall.

In point of fact Ben Hall had nothing to do with this robbery. He just happened to be in the wrong place at the wrong time, though he knew Frank Gardiner and had been directed by 'the Darkie' to ride over into some bushes while the robbery of the second dray took place. But he had been seen, and recognised, if at some 200 yards distance.

When Sir Frederick returned, he was delighted with the information. Or perhaps, with just some parts of it. He may not have been so pleased to learn that Gardiner was laughing at him behind his back, for the theft was more token than substantial. Not that Gardiner was inclined to return the gin. However, the Inspector was pleased to have Ben Hall on his books, and we have to consider why. We have to do our own version of blacktracking, to read the signs where we can, and to deduce a sequence and a direction to follow. Marking the tell-tale evidence of disturbance wherever it has occurred.

For it appears that Ben Hall, who was no bushranger to this point, was in fact very light-fingered with others' stock (he supplied the various butcheries across the goldfields with unmarked cattle), and he was just as self-helping to good-quality horses. At about this time, he had stolen a big-framed thoroughbred, Arabian Star, hitherto the property of none other than Sir Frederick Pottinger.[4] Whether Sir Frederick knew who had done it, or merely suspected it, he seemed to have an otherwise inexplicable preparatory animus against Hall well before he actually encountered him.

He was of course provided with a horse for his police duties. Being an inspector, he would have had the pick of the available mounts, strong and speedy. Those did not necessarily include thoroughbreds, and it was possible for him to ride his own horse, as distinct from a horse of his own choosing. The troopers were mounted on the evolving local breed, the Walers, hard-working, intelligent stayers, and just what was needed when Sir Frederick set out on his marathon searches.

Late in April, Ben Hall had ridden into a local race meeting, and to his astonishment found himself unceremoniously arrested by Sir Frederick, on suspicion of being a member of Frank Gardiner's gang. He was thrown into the lock-up and held there for a week more, and another week again, and again, with Sir Frederick pressing the case that he needed the prisoner to be kept in remand while he looked for evidence.

Because Hall had too many friends in the local community, his trial was transferred from Forbes to Orange. Sir Frederick reasoned that he could not get a jury that would see matters fairly, as distinct from sympathetically. He thought to assist them in coming to an appropriate decision by providing them with pertinent information through the *Police Gazette* of 21 May 1862:

> Found in the possession of Benjamin Hall, a bushranger, a light chestnut mare 16 ½ hands, branded BB near the shoulder, small star; also a saddle and a double-reined bridle, Colonial made; the seat and kneepads are hogskin. The above are now in the possession of the police at Forbes.[5]

Undoubtedly there was some satisfaction in declaring Hall a horse thief. But the community should also know that Hall was a bushranger, and what bushrangers did was rob carriers. They should come to the obvious conclusion.

The jury did just that. To the chagrin of the police, and of Sir Frederick in particular, the jury acquitted him without leaving their seats.[6] They had less confidence in the long sight of the carrier than the close-up vision of the second driver, who denied that Ben Hall was involved.

It took a month before Hall was released, and when he made his way home he found that his horses and cattle had all died because nobody had fed or watered them. He had no savings, and he had no means of support. And his wife had run away with an ex-policeman. Neither she nor the police were at the centre of his affections just then.

Those of us who do not sufficiently consider what we have been told, or shown, doubtless click our tongues at Sir Frederick's part in this. He had gone the worst way about matters, we might think; he was driving Ben Hall into a life of crime. But then, we do not think as the great do. That is why we do not find ourselves in their midst. For consider: it had not been proven that Ben Hall was Frank Gardiner's accomplice in crime, so why not drive them towards each other and then, catch one and you have them both! Each would thereby implicate the other. Ingenious. And in addition, there was the satisfaction of thoroughly discomfiting one who had established himself as utterly annoying. Whichever one of those two captured your interest.

What Sir Frederick did not know was how promptly the bushrangers would exact their own revenge, by pulling off an enormous robbery right inside Sir Frederick's jurisdiction. They would make their fortunes and they would make Sir Frederick a figure of ridicule – though some were of the view that he was well able to do that on his own. Petty, little-minded people, driven by a puerile wish for revenge. Of course he knew what he was doing. He was keeping the gold safe. He was keeping bushrangers at bay.

There were occasional compensations through his employment though, and here again we need to exercise our own tracking skills; we need to read the evidence, again – as so often in Sir Frederick's case – in the record of a trial. At about the time that Ben Hall won his freedom, a case was heard which did not involve the Inspector personally, and yet he was at the very centre of it. A Mr James Torpy, sometimes known as the 'Burrangong patriot,' the publican who had invited Sir Frederick to a ball when he was first appointed to the district, had horsewhipped an ensign from the 12th regiment for his shameful insolence. Torpy had set upon the young soldier as soon as he laid eyes upon him, on a Saturday night at the Diggers' Theatre in Burrangong. That would have been a busy venue, and the attack would have been in full view of an astonished public.

It was revealed in the course of the trial for assault that the young man had sent a copy of Byron's *Don Juan* to a young lady of his acquaintance, which in itself was not a punishable offence, though his selection might have been more circumspect. What he had done was cross out the name Julia throughout the first canto of that notorious poem, and substituted that of the young lady – and that was not only immodest but insolent misbehaviour. It is no wonder that Torpy, enraged, attacked with his horsewhip. The young man himself acknowledged that he too would have resented such a book being sent to his sister or lady friend, should that have happened. But – and this is the curiosity of the case – he insisted that the marked-up poem was not intended for the young lady in question, even though addressed to her. It was to be taken by her to Forbes and given to Sir Frederick Pottinger.

Now what should we make of that? What might Freddy have understood by this modest young woman presenting him with a somewhat scandalous poem, in which she was now personally identified, a poem notorious for its scenes of intimate relations?[7] What kind of trick was being played on her? What, we should be asking ourselves, was the nature of Sir Frederick's connection with her or what was the intended connection? And why had he not been called to the witness stand? What on earth did the young man expect to achieve – was it mere mischief-making?

It is all very curious. One line of explanation might be that for the summer months at least, Forbes could be as climatically invigorating as Madras. Freddy's father had enjoyed the experience of that in his own way, and we should not be surprised if Freddy did so in his turn. Who can say?

It must have been quite unsettling for Sir Frederick. His name had been bandied about yet again. Torpy was required to pay a fine of £5 for taking the law into his own hands, though the consensus was that he was justified in his action. But what of Pottinger, who embodied the law – what satisfaction could he require? That is the inconvenient consequence of greatness. He could not exact his own compensation. The great are expected to rise above such trivialities.

Virtus in ardua indeed. The trouble with a family motto is that you might be expected to live up to it.

At about this time, out towards the frosty flats below the Weddin range and a fair ride out from Forbes, assorted young tearaways – wild colonial boys in the making – joined a few more grim-faced characters in a bush pub run by a man called John McGuire, to plan the biggest gold robbery that had ever occurred in the colonies. A lemonade seller who, by unfortunate timing, happened to be there at the same time, was firmly advised to return to his room, to mind his own business and to stay there.

Frank Gardiner had everything pretty much in hand. He had already begun planting stores in caves hither and thither throughout the mountains, and he had decided who should be in his gang. But it was Ben Hall who identified the exact spot where the gold escort might best be ambushed, where the coach road wound up around a tight gully with massive granite boulders fringing it, and was backed by heavy native pine scrub; and it was Ben Hall who checked that it would leave Forbes as routinely, on a Sunday afternoon.

On 15 June, with the pale winter sun low in the sky, the team of horses slowed considerably as they hauled the weighted coach up long rising sections of the road and then up a tight pinch. This was where Gardiner's gang attacked the gold escort. In relays they concentrated their fire on the coach itself, scaring the horses, which, bolting, soon rolled the coach over. The police were either wounded, or ran for cover and then kept going. The iron strong boxes were smashed open and more than 2700 ounces of gold was seized, approximately 1.5 hundredweight and worth an absolute fortune; together with nearly four thousand pounds in cash – all up, near enough to five million dollars today. It was the biggest robbery in Australia's history to that time, and it had taken just half an hour for them to seize it all, load the packhorses, and gallop off through the enclosing bush to the long shadows and safety of the hills. It would be a few hours before news of the banditry reached the police.

Strangely, this was not the largest quantity of gold that had been carried by the Forbes gold escort. Which might be a way of explaining the rather lacklustre security detail that Sir Frederick had put together. There were five troopers, but four were sitting inside the coach with the gold, and one was up on the top with the driver. There was no accompanying posse of outriders armed to the teeth, nothing of that kind. Easy pickings by ambush; indeed, positively inviting.

When news of the disaster did get through to the police, our hero was decisive and swift in his response, as we may well imagine. Possibly also verbally intemperate. Even though it was evening when they heard of the robbery, armed troopers and citizen volunteers dashed to the site, reaching it late in the night. They had to wait for first light before they could begin a pursuit.

The police were always at a disadvantage in chasing bushrangers, who very often rode stolen racehorses. On this occasion, the odds were more even, because the heavy gold had been stowed in saddle bags on the backs of the coach horses liberated from the overturned coach, and they had already pulled that weight for about 25 miles along the rutted way from Forbes, winding at last past rocky outcrops and towards increasingly steep terrain. Now with their new load they had to gallop across broken ground and through dense pine scrub, then lug their plunder up nearby Wheogo hill. That was hard work, and tiring, and those on racehorses had to moderate their pace. They were not about to let the loot out of their sight.

In order to make matters difficult for an inevitable pursuit party, at some point the gang scattered to confuse their trackers, before eventually meeting at an agreed rendezvous on the top of a hill with clear lines of sight down to any oncoming troopers. Here they set up camp, celebrated their success – maybe with some of Frank Gardiner's purloined stock of gin – and divided their ill-gotten gains into equal shares.

Their tactics had been sound. With the two blacktrackers pointing to diverging tracks, Sir Frederick was quick to see that he must divide his troops. This was where he showed the true measure of his leadership. Time was of the essence. They were hot on the trail of the robbers, but midwinter rain was beginning to settle in, and the hoofprints would soon become obscured. Billy Dargan, knowing this country well, predicted they would head for the hills, if not the mountain range beyond. Sir Frederick thought rather that Gardiner would take off for Victoria, where he had begun his career in crime. Billy rode with a sub-inspector and several troopers, and they followed as best they could one of the trails. The other group, with Sir Frederick leading the way – or perhaps the other blacktracker leading the way and Sir Frederick close on his heels – started off towards the more remote possibility.

It took a couple of days before one of the bushrangers, a look-out, spotted a famous white horse with a black trooper coming up the increasingly steep slope of the hill – Billy Dargan, showing the troopers the way. There was no time to lose. This was an urgency just as pressing as Pottinger's, equal and opposite, like some deep-seated law of nature, and the gang took off in all directions, any direction other than that pre-empted by the search party. Three of them had in fact already left that very morning, taking their share of the spoils with them. For the remainder, some took care of their own portion, some took their banknotes with them but stuffed their share of the gold into the available saddlebags, in the care of Frank Gardiner, and scarpered off down the opposite side of the hill.

Billy Dargan was up to the task. He worked out which tracks to follow, and the troopers followed him. Slowly they began to close the gap behind Frank Gardiner, who was leading the packhorse – he kept prodding it with his rifle, encouraging it with a stick, but the heavily freighted animal just could not go any faster, and eventually Gardiner pulled it into a patch of thick bush close to the Weddin Mountains, hiding it there, to retrieve when the coast was clear. Then he and his accomplices galloped off to the safety of the rocky high country.

Famously, Billy Dargan led the chase and closed in on their quarry. 'Me see um, boss', or words to that effect. He had found the packhorse with 1500 ounces of gold, nearly one-half of what had been plundered. And that is what the sub-inspector triumphantly, if anxiously, brought back to Forbes.

Sir Frederick should not be judged harshly for this. He could have been at the head of the party which claimed that momentous success. He could have chosen to ride in Billy Dargan's shadow. But no, he took on the more difficult challenge. He was in pursuit of the highwaymen themselves. He could leave it to his subordinates to retrieve the stolen gold. With such as himself in the field, in the saddle, this was an eminently sensible use of resources.

While the rain had obscured the fugitives' tracks in the first days, in the current downfall their tracks were as easy to see in the mud as, well, as reading a book. Not necessarily a travel guide. And because Sir Frederick had worked out that they must be headed for Victoria, his first move must be to catch them as they tried to cross the Murrumbidgee. They would have to ford it with their portion of the heavy gold freight, and there were exactly two places where they could manage to do so.[8] Sir Frederick was on to something here. He was every bit as smart as they were. Now the colony should see what he could do. Though he had not quite figured out how to be in those two places at once. Not to worry – a minor detail.

He and his party headed off into the vast waterlogged Riverina plains, straight into driving rainstorms, day after day. Water trickled into their eyes, it ran down their ponchos, it pooled on the ground, and their horses' hooves stuck in the mud. Under his cape Sir Frederick was in proper uniform, including his sabre, in case of necessity, but also displaying his authority (when the rain stopped), in case of a different necessity. On and on they plodded, with steely will and grim determination, and not much else. They had set out from Forbes in the first place with very few supplies, even without much money to buy supplies. They had no change of clothing. They had to hope for assistance from the very occasional homestead.

It was miserable. He was not accustomed to this. We should remember he had never lived in Ireland.

As they headed further and further out, they remained out of touch with what the other party had accomplished. And the rest of the world remained out of touch with them. Days, then weeks, passed by, and a small note of alarm began to sound in various news items. What might this silence portend? What could have happened? Sir Frederick had given evidence in the past of his doggedness, so it was at first presumed he would suddenly reappear with prisoners securely handcuffed to their saddle pommel. Or his. But what if some untoward disaster had happened? If a follow-up party were sent out, would that not serve to demean the intrepid Inspector's skills? It was a worrying time.

As Sir Frederick approached the Murrumbidgee, it was a worrying time for him too. If it had been summer, he might have realised that he was chasing a mirage; for while they had followed a direction, they had found very little in the way of fresh tracks. That made them uncertain, though Sir Frederick's logic remained infallible. And as he thought about it – and what else was there to do in the circumstances? – he became more and more convinced that Frank Gardiner had played no part in the robbery. When at last he did reach an outpost of civilisation, he communicated that opinion to his superiors. If Gardiner were not involved, then there would be no reason for continuing the pursuit towards the southern colony. The logic of his analysis is irrefutable. So they turned themselves about, at what is now known as Hay, to begin the long journey back, a trek of some 400 kilometres.

We have to admit that he was right, in a manner of speaking. Frank Gardiner was not ahead of him, and to keep going in the wrong direction was a waste of time. It might be tempting to jeer at him, and point out that Frank Gardiner was indeed involved in the robbery, and that he was right back where he had been all along, at Sir Frederick's point of departure. But that would be to ignore the salutary example the Inspector had been providing, of the relentlessness of police pursuit in the very foulest of weather.

A week after they had turned about, along a lonely road through dense scrub they came up to three young men mounted on the very best of horses, thoroughbreds, and each leading another horse, one of which had a heavy load. And those of you who were jeering just now, what do you think of this? They were none other than one of Gardiner's gang, Johnny Gilbert, together with his brother, and another of the bushrangers. Where is the mockery now? Sir Frederick had been right all along, it is just that he was ahead of the thieves, not following them. Ahead of them, did you mark that?

When Sir Frederick happened to comment appreciatively on the quality of Gilbert's horse, it occurred to him to ask for proof of ownership, just as a policeman does. Gilbert, standing up in his stirrups and pretending to look for a receipt in his pockets, edged his horse away towards the side of the road, then with a touch of his spurs he was off like greased lightning, the sort that the troopers had been seeing rather too much of lately. When he was out of the range of pistol shot, he wheeled around to see what would happen: his two mates were handcuffed and searched; and a sack with 13 or 14 pounds of gold and £150 in cash that could not be accounted for was taken into custody.

Slowly Pottinger's party made their way back towards Forbes, with a trooper leading the prisoners and Sir Henry and another leading the packhorses. Then, several days later – as though destiny was attempting some counterbalancing compensation – out of the scrub burst three men on foot, wearing what might almost be thought of as the Eugowra gang uniform: red shirts, scarves, blackened faces. And firing double-barrelled shotguns. The policeman in the front was thrown off his rearing horse, he lost his gun, and his horse cantered off into the bush.

From the other side, four men dressed in the same manner stepped out and opened fire, one of them saying 'I know you, you bastard Pottinger, I'll put a pill through you, you bloody bastard!'[9] Is it any wonder that Sir Frederick took offence at the uncouth overfamiliarity of this colonial trash? That was no way to address a peer of the realm. Well, one who was very nearly such a peer. Close enough to impress a damned colonial scruff anyway. And no doubt the fellow thought he was clever in identifying the Inspector, even one wearing a poncho. The sabre was a giveaway.

It was Gardiner of course. Johnny Gilbert had raced all the way back to the Weddin mountains hideout, raised the alarm, and they had calculated with even more unerring accuracy than Sir Frederick which way he must travel on his way back to Forbes.

Freddy may never have lived in Ireland but he could get into a right paddy good and lively, even without a billiard cue handy. The two officers were not going down without a fight – indeed, it never entered Pottinger's head that he might go down at all. They were on horseback and held the advantage. They could wheel and turn and withdraw out of range of pistol shot and then come charging in again, and again, but eventually the point came where they ran out of ammunition. At which stage, they recognised, as once did another knight, Sir John Falstaff, that discretion was the better part of valour, and galloped off to a nearby homestead. 'They were pretty quick about it, covering the twenty kilometres in just forty minutes.'[10]

There you go again, dear reader, suspecting a failure of spirit when in fact we should admire the sterling qualities of one who had been in the saddle for weeks and weeks. You win yourselves no esteem with your own mean-spiritedness. They had kept blazing away while they had a bullet to spare. Then to be able to ride away like that, why it is worth a round of applause. Likewise for the horse. Besides, Pottinger had the captured loot with him. Good man.

It is curious that nobody was wounded in all this melee – nobody on either side, yet pistols were banging and barking, bullets were whizzing about, gunsmoke was coiling about everywhere ... Maybe that is why everyone missed their mark. Nobody laughed at the bushrangers for wasting their ammunition.

The press had a field day. Once such a large part of the stolen gold had been recovered, they began to mock Sir Frederick for having gone off in completely the wrong direction:

> A very good farce might be made of the details of Pottinger's pursuit of Gardiner – riding the tails off no end of horses, galloping hundreds of miles through the bush in quest of a man who was probably never away from the locale of the Lachlan. Scott's haunted huntsman was nothing to Pottinger chasing his prey; yet Burns' Tam O' Shanter with the witches after him, rode no quicker than Pottinger when, having come up with some of the marauders, he galloped ten miles in forty minutes with a knocked up horse, to get away from that 'deadly fire' which hurt nobody, but was sufficient to terrify the baronetted blue bottle into parting with a couple of prisoners.[11]

Despite that facetiousness, and despite questions about Sir Frederick's indisputable bravery, the papers had involuntarily conceded an important point, that he was to be thought of alongside other elevated literary figures, a character larger than life. Surely that is what we would want to take away from this passage, for example?

Others, and more damaging perhaps because these were among the leading metropolitan papers, rejoiced in the amusement that Sir Frederick was supplying. They could afford to play up the ridicule because bushrangers with real bullets were hundreds of miles away.

Their point though, was that Freddy was even further away. The *Empire*, which had carried the line of incredulity right from the start, chortled away at the imagined vision of Pottinger crashing through the bush and en route to Adelaide. That, after all, was the direction in which he was known to have been heading:

> An old German shepherd on the confines of South Australia was last night enjoying his meerschaum outside his hut door, when suddenly a troop of horsemen in full career came dashing through the forest, and disappeared into the darkness thereof. 'Ach!' exclaimed the shepherd starting up with horror; 'Mein Gott! Die Wurten Jager!' But he was mistaken! The wild huntsman and his band have not yet resolved upon emigrating from the banks of the Rhine, and the course of justice in that sluggish land has hitherto saved those disorderly personages from transportation. No! It was neither a spirit hunt nor a wolf hunt. It was only a band of enthusiastic bobbies engaged in that most interesting of all field sports – the chase of the wild-goose.
>
> It was Pottinger! Many a weary day and night had elapsed since he set forth on his terrible ride, and still he was hard at it! Several of the most serviceable horses had already lost their tails, having proceeded at a pace which

> rendered it impossible for those appendages to follow. The woods and scrubs are roused from their loneliness by the galloping of steeds, the waving of plumes and the clattering of sabres. Night and day the hot pursuit goes on. The newly espoused blackfellow abandons his Mary in affright. The kangaroo-rat peeps out of a log, and goes back again. The bandicoot cuts like a lamplighter over the dry leaves, and the 'possum runs up a gum tree. Still the wild chase-the wild-goose chase goes on. There is a rumour that Sir Pottinger got news by telegram from Mount Gambier, that a great billiard-match was going on at King George's Sound, and Ocean alone can pull him up before he gets there. But Spencer's Gulf will stop him, and a battery of artillery, under telegraphic instructions two days ago sent to Adelaide, is waiting there to sound the recall.[12]

How cruel, how thoughtless and ignorant – Pottinger, an enthusiastic bobby! Why, he had just fought off that ambush by a pack of bushrangers, outnumbered seven to two, and he had captured the stolen gold. What more could anyone ask of him? But ask it they did. They wanted arrests.

Regrettably, Pottinger and his deputy had neglected to think of their dazed companion wandering about in the scrub without his own horse, and without his pistol. Come nightfall, they returned to the site of the ambush, found him looking for them, and in the next days they cautiously made their way back ever closer and closer to Forbes, eventually sending a message through to Lambing Flat for a police escort. Gardiner's bushrangers were nowhere to be seen. Just as well, for neither Forbes nor Lambing Flat was guarded in the interim. The local citizenry did not fail to give their opinion about that. You would have thought that it was crucial to guard the gold, but no, they sought only to safeguard their own interests. It is embarrassing to record this petty-mindedness.

Though as Sir Frederick had tethered himself to the main prize, that additional protection might well be deemed superfluous.

On his return he could have spent his time raging or sulking at the way the hunt for the bushrangers had turned out, or weltering in self-pity as the press kept up its chorus of mockery at his ineptitude, and at his madcap headstrong charging about all over the place. But that was not his way. No, he would press on immediately with making inroads into the gang's activities. He needed to make some arrests.

He didn't need the Inspector-General, Captain McLerie, to tell him of this. Nor the Premier. Though they did. Anybody could see that was what had to happen now.

The lemonade seller who had retired to the back room when Gardiner and his cohorts planned the great robbery turned up at the police station, looking for reward money for identifying the flash types or enough of them for charges to be laid. If Pottinger couldn't catch his man – let us be careful and correct here, if Pottinger couldn't hold on to his man – then he could buy the information that would lead to him, or them. And when he had seized half the gang, he could lean on the weakest of them with the offer of parole or leniency to give evidence against the others. So he resumed his strategy of requesting each week that his suspects be remanded for a further week while he sought more evidence.

As the weeks turned into months, Pottinger gradually added to the number of suspects he held in custody. No one was sure exactly how many were in the gang, and besides they obviously were aided and abetted by any number of ne'er-do-wells especially in the Wheogo-Weddin area, Ben Hall country. Better safe than certain, in the circumstances – better to throw the whole lot in prison. That was how to get rid of the riff-raff. One way and another Pottinger and his troopers managed to fill the Forbes lock-up with low-life characters who all knew each other very well indeed, and who were mainly from that one extended troublesome locality.

That was where Frank Gardiner's lady love had her hut too. Here was an opportunity, obviously a prospective lure, a honey trap if ever there was one.

XI

PLAYING WITH FIRE

One of those people who are always inopportune ...

—H.H. RICHARDSON, *Maurice Guest*

ON A CLEAR cold August night, even deeper into winter in a region of New South Wales renowned for its chill, Frank Gardiner kept a clandestine rendezvous with Kitty Brown. From time to time she came outside her little cottage for more firewood, and went back in. All was quiet – especially the troopers and their horses. They had been tipped off that this tryst might be in the offing. Not only bushrangers had their informants.

Gardiner had to come down from Wheogo hill under the cover of sizeable timber, and then as that thinned out, through scrub until it opened out into a clearing about her hut. He was an expert bushman and he was always careful; he knew danger might lie out there in the moonlight. He had been walking his horse at a quiet pace, when suddenly Pottinger stepped out from a bush almost right alongside him, pointed his carbine, called on him to halt and at the same time squeezed the trigger. Gardiner should have been dead.

But he wasn't. In the one moment he shrieked, his horse partly reared, he pulled it around and spurred away flat out; and Pottinger roared at his fellow officers to fire, a different kind of shrieking. He had been almost close enough to touch Gardiner, but he had failed to shoot him.[1]

It has been truly observed that history repeats itself, the first time as tragedy, the second time as farce. At least in Pottinger's previous encounter with Gardiner's gang, guns had actually gone off, bullets had whizzed and pinged. Not this time though. His rifle had totally misfired. Sir Frederick could not believe his luck. Nor, we imagine, could Gardiner.

Glinty-eyed readers will note that in subsequent accounts, his carbine is foreshortened to a pistol. A mere detail.

Kitty Brown of course knew nothing about a visit from Frank Gardiner. When the Inspector searched the bedroom in her cottage, he found an apparently sleepy 15-year-old, her young brother Johnny, known as 'Warrigal' – suggesting he had some of the attributes of a wild dog. Sir Frederick was no fool, notwithstanding newspaper commentary to the contrary. We may well imagine his questioning was intense, his search of the premises vigorous. But as he had no grounds other than his deepest suspicions for arresting Kitty Brown, and as she denied that she had been harbouring an outlaw, then he was obliged to withdraw. He took young Johnny with him, to hold him in custody for the time being. Just in case. You never can tell. It had been an effective strategy earlier, and it would serve his purpose again. Besides, someone who looked like the young lad had once been seen with Gardiner.

The press, when they got wind of it, and the public too, enjoyed his discomfiture – the moment in the bush, not the bedroom. Many took a sardonic view of the matter. In measured tones the *Burrangong Courier* reflected mournfully on the persistent disappointment which met Sir Frederick's heroic efforts: 'Some men are born to luck while others have generally to contend with unfavourable circumstances and unforeseen accidents. We fear that Sir Frederick is one of the latter class'.[2]

You cannot be altogether sure whether this melancholy estimation is mock serious or not. Editors of the day rarely mastered their irony, resorting more confidently to sarcasm or farce, as we have seen. But let us suppose this summation was kindly meant: could there have been any more sympathetic appreciation?

Whereas some wit from the hoary heights of the Australian alps – from the Snowy River if we were to take his pseudonym at face value, a terrain colder by far than the district Sir Frederick was attempting to monitor – submitted a ballad to the *Sydney Morning Herald*, the very bastion of respectability, and where Sir Frederick might have anticipated a modicum of support. But no, this missed opportunity of taking the colony's most wanted man was so incredible as to be laughable:

> Still gleam'd the light through the shades of night, and still
> the pale moon shone,
> But no Ranger came to cheer the dame as she sat by the
> light alone;

The warriors bold were freezing with cold, and thought it
was time to start,
When the echoing beat of a horse's feet sent the blood in
a rush, to the heart!

At gentle speed, on snow-white steed, and singing a
joyous song,
To the twinkling light in the shadowy night the Ranger
rides along;
A stalwart man was he to scan, and flush'd with ruffian
pride,
For in many a fray he had won the day, and the New
Police defied!

Up started then Sir Fred. and his men, with cock'd
carbine in hand,
And call'd aloud on the Ranger proud, on pain of death,
to 'stand!'
But the Ranger proud, he laughed aloud, and bounding
rode away,
While Sir Frederick Pott, shut his eyes for a shot, and
miss'd – in his usual way.

His warriors then, like valiant men, with their carbines
blazed away,
The whistling lead on its mission sped, but whither none
can say;
For the snow white steed, at gentle speed, bore the
Ranger from their view,

And left Sir Fred, to return to bed, – there was nothing
else to do.[3]

The poem delighted one and all, with the probable exception of Sir Frederick. It seemed to sum up his perennial ineptitude perfectly. It laid no blame, it did not accuse him of lacking courage. The attempted ambush had been well planned and well executed, until the crucial moment itself. That misfire was hardly Sir Frederick's fault, though. His mischance, yes. Does that amount to a character flaw?

That was good thinking to keep the horses well away from the cabin, so that their restlessness might not alert Gardiner to the presence of the police. But who would have imagined those lying in wait might have to pursue the bushranger when his horse bolted? That too was a consequence of the misfire, and he escaped easily.

The damage was done. Who would take Freddy seriously now?

The *Lachlan Miner* for one did not attempt to hide its contempt:

> The cowardly conduct of Sir F. Pottinger, who commanded the police on the occasion, requires no comment; there can be but one opinion on the subject. His own evidence condemns him as utterly unfit for the office he holds, and he richly merits instant dismissal.[4]

Harsh, but there you are – that was what people were thinking.

Neither the government nor the Inspector-General could afford to ignore the widespread and increasing disrespect. Once again, Freddy did not need his superiors to spur him on to greater efforts, to catch Gardiner at any cost. And to get Hall sentenced while he was about it. That was what he must accomplish if he were to retrieve so much lost ground.

Indeed, he was ahead of them there. He was ahead of 'Snowy River', too, who came up with his masterly little satire just a week after the event proper.

The acid icing on the cake was that this satire was published on the very day he found himself obliged to release Ben Hall, with all charges dropped after the unsuccessful trial. He couldn't take a trick, it seemed. And everyone was taking their own pot shot at him.

His calmness of mind was tested a little further on the following day, when blacktrackers revealed that 'the audacious Gardiner had ridden only a few hundred metres after his narrow escape and, in complete contempt for his opponents, had there dismounted and squatted on his heels against a tree to watch developments at the house.'[5] The fellow had no respect. None of these colonials had any respect. Damn the lot of them.

But Pottinger stuck to his guns – we would expect no less. He rode about everywhere, he made sure everyone could see how tireless he was in pursuit of his duty, how dogged. Better, they all said, if he were actually in pursuit of Gardiner. He received word – he was always picking up tips, though annoyingly they were mostly about minor matters and never led him to the encounters he sought – that Gardiner might be going to make an appearance in Bathurst, or if not Gardiner then a couple of suspicious types from the Weddin mountains. Hall was no longer in the Forbes lock-up, where he belonged, though Pottinger had contrived to keep him there if not indefinitely then for an unconscionably extended detention. Gardiner had been suspiciously quiet since the big robbery. He was bound to make a move soon. Either of these might be planning a visit; or both.

Towards the end of September Pottinger was over in Bathurst, enjoying the hospitality of a colleague, enjoying some few remnant hints of genteel living. His host, Superintendent Morisset, was later to insist in court that Sir Frederick had not overindulged, and that there was no way that he could have managed to get himself sozzled by midnight when he was out on the streets, looking for trouble. Looking for Gardiner.

As with all these occasions, it is difficult to penetrate to exactly what happened. A fracas took place in the street, a bit of rowdiness on a Wednesday night – not a Saturday night, so likely it was less intemperate than it might otherwise have been. A number of young people, including young ladies, had been at a private party, which broke up after midnight, though with some choosing to stay on.

When one of the young men determined to leave, another of the partygoers ran after him, to encourage him to change his mind. There was some tugging and pulling and doubtless raised voices carrying into the respectable streets of Bathurst, because others of the party were out there too, shoving and jostling and trying to hold the participants – when into their midst strode none other than Sir Frederick. The big Inspector grabbed the would-be spoilsport and shook him and told him to stop struggling, to be quiet or he would put a bloody bullet into him – and held his pistol to the throat of the killjoy.

Given Sir Frederick's record with guns, perhaps that was in fact no very dismaying threat. But what we can see here, and it is deeply distressing to see it, is that Sir Frederick was becoming roughened by his time among the colonials. We cannot imagine him speaking like that in Belgrave Square. We cannot imagine him talking like some lowly corporal in the Guards. And once he had learned to mouth plums, not at Eton either. The man was being worn down by his antipodean experience. His polish, his cultivation, was being abraded. He was beginning to forget himself. Unlucky man!

For this all came out in court – yes, Sir Frederick was back in court and in the papers again. He had done none other than to try to keep the peace, as was his proper responsibility. But he had been taken to court charged with assault. He had hurt the plaintiff's nose, and he had seized him by the throat. He had been overly officious. He had been intimidating. He had called him a damned young wretch.

Let us not overlook the pertinent detail, he had been effective.

At issue was a salient point. All the witnesses affirmed that while Sir Frederick had identified himself by name, they could not remember him saying he was an inspector of police. He had tried to enter the house where the party had been held, but the indignant hostess had shoved him out. When he challenged the young man, who was being retrieved to continue at the party, and seized him by the throat too, Pottinger had asked him, no, he had challenged him with 'don't you know who I am?', and had unwisely left himself open to the regrettable retort 'no, nor don't care'. That exchange was somewhat terse because while Sir Frederick had the young man by the throat, this had meant a counterattack was possible. The young man had seized Freddy's substantial beard and began shaking it. Unfortunately for his dignity, if not his reputation, this took place in front of 12 or 15 people, some from the unravelling party but, what with all the noise and hullabaloo, some from neighbouring houses too.

The trouble with the colonials was a total want of respect. And with it, an overly intrusive interest in any affray.

It seems from the court report in the press that Sir Frederick was more excited than any of the partygoers: 'I cannot say if defendant was drunk, but I should think he was from his appearance; he was excited'.[6] In which regard, we read with sympathetic understanding the determination of his own witnesses to assert one after the other that he was sober. While that might lead us to think they did protest too much, the magistrates understood their duty. They did not see the necessity of a long procession of identical testimony, and dismissed the case.

Whereupon the other young man, the beard-shaking one, seeing which way the wind was blowing, withdrew his complaint against Sir Frederick.

We have to consider why Sir Frederick had presumed to patrol the streets of Bathurst when it had its own police force and superintendent, albeit a recent appointment. Superintendent Morisset[7] was experienced, he had form from Queensland, where he had overseen a number of 'dispersals' of tribes. It remains unclear what benefit this accomplishment might have contributed to the Bathurst region.

From what we can deduce, it looks as though Inspector Pottinger had taken it upon himself to pursue the Weddin mountains brotherhood; and that suggests various reflections upon his character. He had already shown himself to be impetuous and indeed headstrong. This further episode however hints at a degree of pushiness. It is as though he had no wish to share the glory of capturing Gardiner. That mild criticism is painful to concede. But then again, the great are not to be measured against our more ordinary comprehension. For it is not impossible, indeed it must be considered, that Sir Frederick knew his proper destiny. Gardiner should be his.

Hall was already marked as his too. That damned scoundrel was about to get his comeuppance.

By definition, it requires a steady nerve to persist single-mindedly in one's duty. When Sir Frederick had been forced to release Ben Hall, that was because an informer had named others of the Eugowra robbery but Hall was not among them. The informer stubbornly refused to name his close friend, instead referring to him as someone he did not know, and had never seen, 'Billy'. Without the tell-tale evidence, Pottinger had no grounds for keeping Hall in the cells. At least he had three or four of the others, and he brought them before the Forbes magistrate, who referred them to a fuller investigation at Bathurst.

Bathurst was not kind to Sir Frederick. When the prisoners were paraded before the Bench, the magistrate there admonished him for bringing manacled prisoners into court. Another

Bathurst humiliation. Their irons should have been struck off in the yard, the magistrate said. But at least Sir Frederick had brought his suspects in. He was not so much over-zealous as ultra-careful. A pity the magistrate did not acknowledge his forethought – another of those pompous country magistrates no doubt. The entire system of justice in this infernal country needed radical overhauling. In the meantime, he would do what he could to at least ensure the criminal rabble were brought to justice. He could do no more than that.

Given such widespread interest in the Eugowra escort case, and in the crime, the court ordered the prisoners to be referred to a Special Criminal Commission in Sydney, to be held in February. This move for a showcase trial might have had a political benefit for the government, but the decision was unpopular in the southern and western districts, for the witnesses and the friends and relatives of the accused had to traipse all the way to the capital, and maintain themselves for its duration. Sir Frederick, of course, one of the more important witnesses, could stay at his club, the Victoria Club in Castlereagh Street, at that time of year a pleasant stroll away from the courthouse.

The trial proper proved less than satisfactory; indeed, that seems to have been the case more often than not in the New South Wales courts. Not that his time at the Croydon assizes had been any more congenial. For four days the lawyers kept digging away into the evidence, and in the end the jury could not reach a unanimous decision. Those who had made the long journey in support of their own were elated, as apparently were many of the urban spectators, far too sympathetic for their own good; those who had stayed at home and had a vested interest in the establishment and maintenance of law and order all shook their heads. The trial should have been held at Bathurst.

The prisoners were not released, however. Sir Frederick was not to be let off scot-free either; he had his own tribulation, if not exactly a trial. With the jury having been discharged, he had a moment or two of leisure, the weekend to himself, a rare event. Late on the Saturday evening, he was strolling down King Street in the city, or in Pitt Street, or he was smoking quietly outside his club in Castlereagh Street, when, as the press reported, he was assaulted from behind by three, or five, or eight unknown assailants; or he was punched in the face. The reports were all at variance.

Indeed, it could well have been he was assaulted at all those locations. Astonishing as it is to us as we closely follow the stellar course of his career, he was not universally admired. Indeed, we ought to entertain the possibility that there was a spate of violent assaults, with poor Sir Frederick ambushed again and again in the murky streets of Sydney – in some accounts he was knocked sprawling into a muddy gutter. Just like Sir Frederick himself, we don't know exactly what happened. He was the only witness, and yet he did not witness what actually occurred. Though according to some accounts of this stirring episode he saw young fellows further up the street laughing at his discomfiture. Even at this distance in time we share his confusion, and his pain.

He reported the event, which is the only way we know the little that we do. We do know that he was not severely wounded, for all the reports reassure us of that. Good man,

Freddy. But we need to consider why this attack occurred. It may have been pure chance: he was unwise to be out on his own at such a late hour on a Saturday night. Or it might have had something to do with his conduct and his testimony at the Special Commission, and the popular support for the accused.

The *Empire*, which we have to admit did not sufficiently admire Sir Frederick's sterling efforts, unsurprisingly offered a different interpretation. Note, an interpretation. The *Empire* was not in the habit of inventing facts, so their report has to be considered on its own merits.

Their account of this episode considered what could have been a motive for the assault. Sir Frederick, said the *Empire*, had regularly proved himself a sufficiently harmless policeman, who offered no threat to those of the miscreant class. It was in the interest of those who offended against the law to keep him in his office, not to attempt to remove him from it. Some other explanation needed to be advanced. And one lay ready to hand.

On that very evening, a hospital fete had been under way in Hyde Park, quite close to the zone of these irregularities. The *Empire* remembered that Sir Frederick was of an adventurous and social mind and (so it was reported), on this occasion:

> distinguished himself by closely scrutinising the ladies under their bonnets – a piece of baronet-policeman impertinence, which was so resented by certain young fellows – brothers and sweethearts mayhap – that they took the first opportunity of giving the beau a jostling outside, said to be considerably less than he deserved.[8]

Other newspapers picked up this detail too. They evidently recognised plausibility here. And whether or not we want to lend credence to it, whether or not he was actually ogling young ladies, we have to allow an aspect of his private character has surfaced in this account; whereas his public character is perfectly well displayed through his policing activities. Possibly he had been spending too much time in the bush and it was not serving him well.

Sir Frederick's misfortunes grew and grew. As proof incontrovertible that his presence was a necessary deterrent to criminal activity, while he was away in Sydney giving his evidence, the unruly colonials had committed another outrage. Up in the country they had raided the new Pinnacles lock-up, established to maintain the presence of the law in what had been a pocket of lawlessness. Two troopers stationed there had absented themselves briefly, to take their breakfast at a nearby inn. While they were out of the way a pair of bushrangers entered the station, took all the guns, powder and ammunition, police uniforms, saddlebags and bridles, and a horse. The assumption was that this was Gardiner's doing. What might they want with police uniforms? And how astonishing, how impudent, to have stuck up a police station![9]

It was Ben Hall, in fact. And McLerie could not wait for Pottinger to get back to his post. The entire police force was becoming a laughingstock.

When a second trial over the Eugowra gold robbery by the Special Criminal Commission followed a fortnight later – a continuing expense for those benighted supporters from over the mountains, as well as the witnesses – the lawyers were able at last to persuade the jury to come to an agreed verdict. Three of the four accused were pronounced guilty; the fourth man, the inn-keeper McGuire, who thought he was to go free was in fact remanded to the debtor's yard, as he had stood bail for an acquaintance who failed to turn up for his own trial. Unfortunately, having been kept so many months in remand, McGuire had not the wherewithal to pay it. The system was determined to make a point to those who had any connection, however remote and indirect, with bushranging activity.

And likewise, with the judgement pronounced on the other three defendants, another stunning action took place, again at the wayward part of the world where Sir Frederick was not. The officer in place up there, Inspector Norton, had gone out on a search for bushrangers, arranged to meet his main body of troopers at a certain place and found himself instead met by the very quarry he sought, a large number – the news reports excitedly said 14 or 15 of them. Given those odds, Norton inevitably ran short of ammunition in the consequent shoot-out; given those numbers, it is extraordinary again that nobody was hurt. Norton had to surrender.

His blacktracker escaped though (also unwounded) and made his way back to the town, reporting on what had happened; and further, reporting that if the sentence pronounced against the three criminals in Sydney were carried out, Norton would be hung too.

Telegrams flew back and forth all over the country. A police inspector captured? And held to ransom? Who was running this country? A large detachment of troopers, some three dozen, was immediately despatched to the Lachlan. No such numbers were sent up from Sydney whenever one of the general population was seized by rogues. That discrepancy was remarked.

An equal number of local volunteers were sworn in as special constables. What a to-do. So much excitement. And then Inspector Norton showed up. He had been held for only three hours. The detail that slowly emerged is that he had been mistaken for another trooper. He too was given a message to take back to the police station: had he been Sir Frederick Pottinger, they would have shot him 'dead as a crow'.[10]

In the meanwhile the whole district had been up in arms; and Sydney likewise grew over-excited. Newspapers huffed and puffed about the disgrace of this incident. Then, when reports of Norton's safe return began to spread, second thoughts began to appear. What had he been about, extracting so many police from Forbes, and leaving the town unprotected? How could he have run out of ammunition without actually wounding any of that numerous contingent? And how come not one of them had managed to ping him – were they not really trying to take him down? Lastly, why did news of his capture constitute grounds for promotion?

There was just one man to return everything to order, one man to re-establish the peace, one man to restore faith in the authority of the law. Not Inspector Battye, but Inspector Sir Frederick Pottinger – with a sore head.

He had no time to waste. He was out on the field almost at once, out with Billy Dargan showing him the way, leading him to the very spot where Norton had been shot at, protected by a tree. The bullet holes were fresh, and large, and deep. As Billy studied the hoofmarks in that vicinity, he identified a fresh set of marks cutting across the scene, and that was enough for Sir Frederick. Off they went – they could even see way ahead a horse galloping at a furious rate; and that was what they found tethered to a hut at the Pinnacles diggings, all of a sweat. Its girths were a pair stolen from the police station when that lock-up was raided. Inside the hut were a pair of no-hopers who could not or would not assist the Inspector, which only served to convince him that their fugitive was somewhere nearby.

They found him; or they found his tracks to where he had been. These led to the top of an abandoned mine shaft, with a ladder going down about 60 feet; and no tracks led away from the shaft. Sir Frederick inquired of the void whether anyone was down there; and again; and again, with slightly less courtesy each time, until in the end he threatened to throw burning timbers into the shaft, to smoke out whoever was down there – like a possum out of its hollow. Sir Frederick was going native.

The ungentle threat was enough. A disembodied voice called up from the pit of despair and in time someone began a slow ascent. As soon as his head came up over the rim, Billy recognised him as one of those who had attacked him and Inspector Norton, and one of those he had chased at the time of the police station robbery. Ben Hall was implicated, too. That was enough for Freddy.

John McGuire later related the story of the police almost catching Hall in the hut, where the two no-hopers were loafing about. When the troopers' approach was announced by the dogs barking, Hall jumped on his old stock horse and dashed off for a mile (he too was narrowly missed when another tracker fired at him from behind an outhouse), and then slipped off to hide behind a tree. The old stock horse galloped off by itself, as stock horses are wont to do thinking they are after stock, and the troopers, headed by Sir Frederick, chased after it. The police hunted about, and at the end of the day camped in a river bend.

> That night Ben boldly essayed to secure Sir Frederick's horse, which was a valuable mount. He waited till such time that he thought the troopers would all be asleep, then tried to snatch the horse. But they [the other horses] ran around so much that the noise of the rattling hobbles awakened the men, who got up to ensure there was nothing amiss. Ben saw them coming and slipped behind a tree, and kept walking around it as the police were passing. It was an exciting time for the outlaw, but the darkness was in his favour. And when the troopers returned to Sir Frederick and reported that nothing was wrong – that an opossum must have frightened the horses – Ben quietly caught the charger and slipped away with him.
>
> Imagine Sir Frederick's disgust next morning at finding his mount missing, and having to ride back to Forbes on Ben Hall's old screw of a stock horse![11]

That would certainly have been enough to fire up the Inspector. He invariably kept a very good horse.

The next day, or maybe the day after that, depending on how much allowance you make for telegrams, Sir Frederick and his troopers rode out to Ben Hall's property and burned down his cottage.[12] Hall had not been able to keep up with the terms of his leasehold, so that in point of fact it was no longer his; but Sir Frederick wanted to ensure that his claim was wholly erased. He no longer lived in his hut, though two women did, one said to be Ben Hall's paramour. That was not an arrangement to be encouraged, not if the intention was to establish some respectability in the neighbourhood. They and their furnishings were unceremoniously bundled out into the winter rain, with no more shelter than a piece of calico.

It was a fierce and decisive action, but what we might expect from a great man, fierce and decisive himself. The whole Wheogo–Weddin precinct housed an infestation of rogues. Well, they should be cleared out.

And that was that.

It shocked the entire community. No arrangement had been made for the woman in question. It was a brutally ruthless operation. But satisfying.

Yet in common with the emerging pattern of Freddy's misfortune – the poor timing of the distinctive events in his life – this was just when that wretched lad he had found in Kitty Brown's four-poster bed, and who had been confined to the logs in Forbes, 'the Warrigal' as he liked to call himself – at just this time, his malingering and pretence at illness became rather more serious. Indeed, there was a clamour to have him given medical attention, and as that could not very well happen inside the prison, he was carried to the White Hart Hotel, where the services of the medical profession would be more readily available.

Sir Frederick's report on the matter was read in the Legislative Assembly. Young Walsh had been discharged from custody, on bail, then taken in again on suspicion of bushranging, and then a subsequent charge of horse stealing. He had been recovering quite well under medical supervision (Freddy had not conceded that Walsh was unwell with 'colonial fever' in the first place) when Walsh's mother effected his removal to the public house. That is not actually what the magisterial enquiry into Walsh's death established; the removal had been initiated by the sergeant in charge, and the mother arranged the transfer. Freddy's was a small harmless massaging of the record, no doubt. A second Sir Henry.

Presumably Sir Frederick had agreed to this; he would not let Frank Gardiner's brother-in-law slip away that easily. The boy was treated at the White Hart by, in the Inspector's view, some quack, and within a matter of days he was dead. That, to Pottinger's mind, proved the doctor's ineptitude.[13] He ignored the presence of a second doctor who had attended Walsh in the prison.

Some, who just could not see that Sir Frederick had behaved with the most rigorous adherence to the law, pointed out that young Walsh had been given a foreshortened life sentence yet had never been brought to trial for any offence. Some raised the spectre of manslaughter or murder. Sir Frederick had been vindictive – yet on his own testimony he had listened to a mother's wishes. Not the sergeant's. What more did they want?

The population at large was not satisfied with that, they wanted an official enquiry. They could see no justification for such a long incarceration in unhealthy conditions. They could not see that he had been used as possible bait to lure the still-elusive Gardiner out of hiding. Or that he had served a key role as a bush telegraph. Of course Sir Frederick had his reasons. He just did not care to share them. And because they could not see as he could see, then this must have been about the time that Sir Frederick was burned in effigy, a man of straw.[14]

XII

KICKING AGAINST THE PRICKS

Do not forget the whip.

—FRIEDRICH NIETZSCHE

BEING SUCH PUBLIC figures, the two Pottingers, father and son, regularly found themselves at the centre of parliamentary debate. Their energetic actions fomented discussion. Sir Henry's exploits in Hong Kong had focused the attention of Westminster, the mother of parliaments; and in Sydney, Sir Frederick was likewise noticed in what would later become known as 'the bear pit', where the Legislative Assembly on Macquarie Street ruminated on matters of local interest and consequence. As a protégé of the Premier, Sir Frederick, and his accomplishments, and his character, were resolutely protected from any unpleasantness by Opposition Members.

A number of those across the Chamber remained steadfastly critical, and loudly so, of the new Police Act. They were particularly hostile to the introduction of a quasi-military principle of centralisation. Again and again they remarked on the absurdity of troopers out in the country having to refer back to their superiors and await approval for some new line of action in the pursuit of bushrangers. They were sarcastic about the incompetence of troopers unfamiliar with the region they were meant to be patrolling, and they were scathing about the weight of equipment the troopers had to carry when fleetness in pursuit was the highest priority. They were equally scathing about shiny buttons glinting in the sunlight and advertising their approach. They brushed aside Sir Frederick's written assertion that whenever his men were out in the bush scouting for miscreants, they dressed in ordinary clothing, without all the old paraphernalia, and presented themselves as much like bushrangers as they could.

Freddy may not have descended quite that far. On the evidence of old photographs, out of uniform he managed to look more like a successful squatter.

His critics in the House, as in the press, continued especially unhappy about the 'torture, sufferings, and death of young Walsh ... [who] was killed by inches; his head shaved, and died raving mad. What will Sydney people and the colony at large think of English justice, and mercy, and liberty', for that had all been premised on the evidence of 'witnesses' known to be corrupt.[1]

Incompetence was one thing, injustice was another; and inhumanity was of course wholly unacceptable. Sir Frederick's most persistent critic in the House, J.J. Harpur, Member for Patrick's Plains in the lower Hunter, made it his mission to speak to the reprehensibility of the Inspector's actions, and in particular to remind the House of the burning of Ben Hall's hut. Not that he was speaking up for the rights of bushrangers, not at all; and he could not be said to hold the romanticised attitude of his brother, the poet Charles Harpur, who only a few years previously had published a somewhat overpitched play about bushrangers.[2] But he was determined that the procedures followed by the police should be both just and humane. He would have nothing to do with the eviction of women and children into the cold dark night. And so he kept up his running attack, characterising actions such as Pottinger's cowardly and inhumane.

He questioned Sir Frederick's veracity too. He cited a number of instances in which he maintained Pottinger had behaved shamefully. He read to the House from a letter he had been sent:

> I must tell you about burning of houses and turning women and a baby out in the cold to get shelter under the trees in wet. One of the women is now under the doctor's care, from being out with only a small bit of calico to keep the night air and cold from her and a baby of two months old. That was after Sir Frederick burnt the house and all that was in it. The two women and baby had to stop out in the wet. Sir Frederick and two men were at Hall's house. He burnt the house down and turned the women out. The man (Hall) was only a hundred yards from them on a knocked-up horse. He only galloped a quarter of a mile, and then his horse gave in, and he jumped off and let the horse go. They got the horse, but not the man. Still Sir

> Frederick was riding as good a horse as was in the district; but he acted in his usual way, disputing with the women, instead of going after the bushrangers. That is the way he has always acted, for he has not yet taken a man that tried to get away; and then his excuse is to the Government that the squatters harbour them.

In a postscript his informant added, 'We shall soon think up here that we are in Russia, not in a British colony, for Sir Frederick rules supreme'.[3]

We must allow people to have their own dissentient opinions. Whatever people might think about Sir Frederick's actions, he could point to the successful outcomes of them. Frank Gardiner had not been heard of since his close escape from the Inspector's ambush. He and his white horse had disappeared, together with Kitty Brown. A number of those involved in the Eugowra escort robbery had been brought to justice, either terminally or for a protracted period. In the Lachlan district, for which he held responsibility and where bushranging had been rife, the roads were now almost clear, and safe. That is what he had been appointed to accomplish, and that is exactly what he had accomplished.

Pottinger did not mind about inhumanity, and untruthfulness could be understood or misunderstood in different ways; but he drew the line at cowardice. He was furious, then, at the published report of this particular parliamentary debate. That gallant gentleman, as Harpur called him, meaning exactly the opposite, that gallant gentleman came to Harpur's residence puffing on his cigar and flourishing his horsewhip, and demanded that Harpur retract what he had said in the House. And if not, that he should accompany him to Tattersall's (site of more than a few duels to satisfy wounded honour) and repeat his accusation there.

It was clear that Freddy had intended to use his whip. Harpur stepped right up to him, declined, and suggested Sir Frederick had been wrong to come to him in such a way. Whereupon the intrepid Inspector left and returned soon 'with a friend', meaning he had taken legal advice. He had good reason to back off, as Harpur was a very strong man and an adept in the manly art of self-defence. No sensible ex-Grenadier Guardsman would think to take him on. Harpur could have given a good account of himself, especially as Freddy was without his billiard cue. In all likelihood our dashing hero was advised not to bring his whip this second time, and to put out his cigar.

We are inevitably reminded of his unhappy encounter with Miss Elizabeth Coyle, though the chances are that he did not see the resemblance; or did not choose to remember it.

Meanwhile Harpur had likewise consulted a 'friend', the most adept legal mind in the House, William Bede Dalley; and, given Freddy's imposing himself as he had, he (Harpur) declined to offer any apology. Sir Frederick was welcome to take any complaint to the Supreme Court. We should be cautious about interpreting Sir Frederick's inactivity in that respect as a demonstration of his cowardice. Rather, we should regard him as declining to become entangled in a public stoush with someone he would not wish to meet socially. He was his father's son, without a doubt.

Harpur wrote him a letter, not of apology as some assumed, but restating exactly what he thought of Inspector Pottinger and of the police force. Instead of reappearing with his horse-whip, Freddy, in the view of the *Yass Courier*, left town rather hurriedly, and without answering the letter.[4] The innuendo is unmistakable. That rapid departure had not helped his cause, or not in the public eye, and rather reinforced Harpur's characterisation of him in the House – yet for all we know, he could have been ordered by the Inspector-General to return to his post. The last thing his superiors would have wanted was for Sir Frederick to be called to account again in a courtroom.

In the eyes of his masters, and of the public at large, he was proving more incompetent than inept. Either way, once again an embarrassment. He had failed to take Gardiner, who was nevertheless very quiet – Darkie Gardiner might well have died of unknown wounds, or he might have gone to Victoria, which in New South Wales terms amounted to much the same inglorious end. He was conspicuously inactive. As for the others, Freddy had failed to take Ben Hall, increasingly his *bête noire*. Likewise Johnny Gilbert. Those two chaffed at him like burrs under his saddle.

For Gilbert too had disappeared from sight. Eventually it emerged that he and his brother had determined to 'go straight', more or less, and headed across to the New Zealand goldfields. There, ever-vigilant, Johnny Gilbert had tried to keep his head down, in case he was recognised by Australian diggers trying their luck. One of the tricks he took up was to disguise himself as a woman, which suggests a colourful conception of what might be understood by going straight.

For a start, he was slim and he had no beard, a point Sir Freddy was all too pleased to bring to the world's attention. The Inspector's own prodigious growth had survived that tug-of-war in the backstreets of Bathurst.

Johnny Gilbert was an unprepossessing young damsel. Far from avoiding notice, dressed up like that, he actually drew attention to himself. When you think about it, in presuming that he passed as a fair approximation, his disguise was an unhappy satire upon New Zealand women. In fact, his cross-dressing was more titillating to himself than to anyone else. Like a lumberjack he had a big lumpy jaw; sketches and photographs show him to have a wide mouth, though police reports refer to his laughing grey eyes. Tenniel could have done him justice.

On his own say-so, back in New South Wales Gilbert had ridden into the races on occasion, dressed to kill:

> Now it is well-known here that Gilbert has a good-looking, but effeminate countenance, and a very light figure; consequently, [for a wager] and to gratify his passion for racing sports, he dressed himself in women's clothes, with a lady's riding habit, hat, feather, and veil; and he afterwards boasted … that he saw the whole of the races at Young, and was once so close to the baronet as to touch his horse.[5]

Before we join the chorus of those who jeer, we should consider that Freddy himself was passionate about racing, and was doubtless utterly absorbed in what was happening on the track too. After all, we know he had an eye for horses.

This particular occasion could not have been the three-day race meeting held at Young at the beginning of June 1863. Gilbert was only just back from New Zealand then, and he announced his return with a bang. While some 2000 punters were enjoying their outing, Johnny Gilbert and his gang were making merry in somewhat different circumstances. Sir Frederick created a stir of his own, for he appeared on the racecourse:

> with blankets strapped on before him on the saddle, a quartpot, a pair of hobbles; and a pair of handcuffs, being artistically arranged around other parts of his saddle. His man Friday, in the shape of a black tracker, followed him. The whole, to use a much hackneyed phrase, 'forming an unique sight which must be seen to be believed'.[6]

Freddy had determined on showing himself to advantage. He had chosen to reassure the townspeople that they and their property were safe. He would display the full force of the law. He was there to keep close watch on all that passed in front of him, as everyone knew that the bushrangers found horseflesh an irresistible temptation. And he was properly equipped to head off at a moment's notice in hot pursuit of any offenders.

Which, of course, meant that nobody much was on duty in the town itself. Gilbert and his men took advantage of the nearly empty streets. They relieved individuals of watches and horses and saddles, they robbed stores not a quarter of a mile from the police camp while Sir Frederick maintained his commanding presence at the racecourse, until news of the nearby misdemeanours was brought to him by a messenger – and then, as was his wont, Freddy galloped off at full speed to where the robbers had been. Where else should he gallop, we may ask ourselves? But to the too-critical public, it looked like he was always short of the mark, always trying to catch up. That, unhappily and cruelly, is a policeman's lot. He can only follow a trail after the event. If he has eyes to see. Or a tracker to show the way. In this instance, Freddy did not know just where to head. He could only circle about, scouring the countryside as he called it. But he could do so at to speed.

The winter months were as cold and relentlessly wet as they had been the previous year, less than an ideal climate for bushrangers forced to camp out. It was no wonder that when they could they lingered indoors, for example, when they attacked some of the big homesteads around Carcoar; or whenever they held up a hotel, as for instance at a three-day party in the hotel at Canowindra, where the only policeman in town was detained in amongst the revellers. It was an opportunity for the outlaws to warm up and dry out somewhat – inevitably an extended process, given they had ready access to the bar.

Having discovered that indoors work was more comfortable than out on the road, within days they began a series of raids on well-established properties. The attractions were an ample meal, select wines, a piano for some young lady to play for them, and more often than not a choice of racehorses in the stables. There was rarely any testing encounter with the law. Even when excited messengers arrived at the nearest police camp, the troopers seemed to dawdle somewhat, as though they were not particularly enthusiastic about confronting well-armed bushrangers. The press and the public had nothing but contempt for the force.

Sir Freddy, to give him his due, was not one of these. He always went off at full tilt. Not necessarily to the right place, but he would get there in the end. In a spate of incidents at this time, while Freddy was whizzing about the countryside, station owners were making their own stand against the Hall and Gilbert gang. Famously, Henry Keightley and his wife held out in a furious exchange of bullets, and for once someone actually did get badly wounded – one of the bushrangers, shot through the stomach.[7]

About a fortnight later, Gilbert, Hall and another bushranger, O'Meally, turned up again at the Canowindra Hotel. They knocked on the door at midnight to buy some whisky, but the publican refused to accept their ill-gotten money. The next day, the police came rather close to catching up with them. Early in the morning three draymen had just put their billy on the fire when the bushrangers galloped up to them, and demanded some breakfast, quick. Also feed for their horses.

But at that moment Freddy and his troopers came up the road. The wanted men leapt on to their horses and took off across country. Ben Hall muddied his reputation as a bushman by riding into a swamp. Dismounting, he struggled to extricate his horse. Gilbert and O'Meally stayed each side of him, well-armed; the police, and we have to include Freddy in this, stopped 20 yards from them, firing wildly while Hall gradually pulled his mount free. Then when everyone was ready, off they all went again. The whole farce was reported to the press:

> My informant states that he watched the progress of the belligerents for a great distance, and could observe that the police lost ground at every stride. It has since been made known that the police after a prolonged chase lost sight of the freebooters, as usual, and returned with their horses considerably blown. If these are the actual facts of the case – and there appears no reason for doubting them we have another illustration of the peculiar construction of the New South Wales 'military' police.[8]

Other accounts of this episode indicate that the police had stopped to load their pistols. Well of course – you could hardly exchange fire any other way. When the renowned Pottinger and his men came up to the interrupted breakfast, and were informed that the bushrangers were not far ahead and could be easily overtaken, they stopped for a smoke for 20 minutes.[9] Whether that was true or not, it was a story widely repeated. And we have observed that Freddy was very fond of a cigar. Perhaps the real point was that the police were giving their horses a spell.

About a week later, the three bandits were back at the Canowindra Hotel again, and as on the previous occasion they paid. It was all a bit of a lark apparently. This time, however, when they left they encountered a young man named Hirkett – one with a very good reputation in the district – whom they recognised as having ridden about with Sir Frederick once, trying to hunt them down. He would have to pay a penalty for that. They proposed to march him into the bush and tie him to a tree. But just as this was about to happen, a Superintendent

Chatfield arrived in the village. He set off after them, his black-tracker sighting them from a distance.

The bushrangers took off at a gallop, much like Freddy in fact; and Hirkett's horse, catching the excitement, galloped off with them. That was enough for Inspector Chatfield. It proved Hirkett was a bushranger too. His two troopers were somewhat rough in arresting him, clubbing him and one urging the other to 'kill the b----y wretch!' He was handcuffed and ordered to stay where he was while they went off chasing the bushrangers.

After what was too long an interval, Hirkett began to walk the long way back to Canowindra, thoughtfully carrying with him a loaded pistol one of the troopers had dropped. And that is how matters stood when Sir Frederick arrived on the scene, a little late again but at the right place. When Hirkett said he had been stuck up by the bushrangers, Sir Frederick was magnificent. 'You are a liar, Hirkett', he said: 'which he followed up by the following sentence – "I will give you three chances; either put me on the track of the bushrangers, stand your trial, or go with the bushrangers!"'[10]

That third choice is accepted as what he might have said. Other versions, on the basis of a few dashes, indicate something else unprintable might have been aired. But whatever words were actually spoken, it is simply a thrill to read how Freddy went about his police work; for Hirkett did not demur, he showed Freddy exactly where the bushrangers had gone, and so earned his release.

Chatfield returned about this time and immediately re-arrested Hirkett, locked him up and had him thrown into the Cowra cells the next day.

Some namby-pamby tenderhearted members of the public took umbrage at this behaviour. They thought Superintendent Chatfield and his troopers should not have started shooting at a man just on suspicion. Furthermore, if he was a man under suspicion, why was he left unguarded by the side of the road? Some were more concerned about Freddy:

> Pottinger, who covets a position he can never acquire, degraded the office he fills, by parleying with one whom he confidently believed was connected with the bush-rangers. There was a sad want of that independent dignity which scorns to hold out terms of treaty with those who must be regarded as society's greatest enemies.[11]

He should not have attempted to make a deal with a man who might, for all he knew, have been a miscreant. He should have arrested him.

Obviously, someone had to be censured for the mis-handling of this unfortunate young man. As it turned out, it would be Chatfield; but as a way of the Inspector-General declaring confidence in Freddy, guess who was appointed to investigate the matter? It did not take Freddy long to report that Chatfield's conduct was without blame. As always his duty was to uphold the good name of the police force. Nevertheless, in the end Chatfield would be obliged to resign; not Freddy.

It is a worry though, that Freddy had not seen innocence when it was in front of him, that he was blind to sterling moral character.

On his way back from Cowra to Forbes, he was met by a messenger who informed him of a shoot-out at another property, Goimbla; and maybe four attacking bushrangers had been shot. Station owners were evidently a lot more determined, and a lot deadlier, than either the police or the assailants. That news would have perplexed Freddy just as it excited him. The number of those wretches was being severely culled, and they were being culled on his patch – but *he* hadn't shot them, or captured them. Again.

He was able to identify the one body available for inspection, Johnny O'Meally, shot through the neck. Pottinger knew him well. He had kept him in the lock-up for some weeks, and he had observed him closely during the trial, or trials, about the gold escort robbery. He swore to that identification at a magisterial enquiry held at the property on 20 November, the day following the attack. The fatal mistake made by the bushrangers was in setting fire to the barn of a Mr Campbell at Goimbla, filled with hay but also holding horses. That did not end well for them. The bushrangers, but the horses also. The light of the fire had given Mr Campbell his opportunity – he could see O'Meally quite clearly, and shot him.

Either before the enquiry, or soon after it was completed, many of those in attendance helped themselves to a lock of O'Meally's hair. These souvenirs were on display at every pub and most of the shops in Forbes; the unkind press speculated that Freddy and his troopers had also pocketed memorial samples. They noted that at last Freddy had actually caught up with a bushranger, albeit a dead one, and they awaited with interest his next adventure. 'His next feat of arms is anxiously looked for.'[12]

The serious press, all across New South Wales and in the other colonies too, made the point that private citizens had accomplished what the police had uniformly failed to do. They were exterminating the brutes. That again highlighted police incompetence.

In the days that followed, permission was given for O'Meally to be given a proper funeral. He was interred alongside the grave of Johnny Walsh, which prompted those reporting on the ceremony to remind their readers of how it was that young fellow had died, and who had been responsible for his lamentable incarceration. Freddy could not take a trick. Undoubtedly the lad would have become a bushranger before long and so was it not a benefit to have him out of the picture too? Nobody seemed inclined to take up that view of the unfortunate circumstances. All they would concede is that his death was the only practical result of Sir Frederick's military operations.

Gilbert and Hall had taken off. They were spotted by a tollkeeper when they needed to cross the river at Payten's bridge, not all that far from Eugowra. They tendered a pound note for the two shillings toll, and they watched him closely when he went to get their change. That done, they cantered off, into the wet weather ahead – they were wearing ponchos, which concealed them pretty well.

Freddy, it will be remembered, used the same wet-weather gear, and found that hindered his movements on occasion. When, we wonder, would he ever had come near enough to a bushranger to use his sabre?

XIII

THE SILLY SEASON

No great man lives in vain.

—THOMAS CARLYLE

IN THE PARLIAMENTARY cycle, regularly - meaning the turn of the year - there comes a time when nothing much of consequence is before the House. That is exactly when dull reports are dropped on the table, when Members' attention wanders elsewhere, and the inner sanctum of a club seems so much more inviting. At the beginning of 1864, that is, when a report on criminal activity in New South Wales over the previous 18 months was presented, and for want of any other fare, the Members pored over the evidence of so much unhappy and costly disruption to the peace. Given that the thrust of the report was to quantify matters, it is pertinent that Freddy's name nevertheless managed to surface, again.

He did not exactly monopolise the attention of the House, but he engaged their thinking. In himself, he seemed to summarise all that was wrong with the way the police were doing their duty; though for others he was a glowing example of dedication and attention to duty. Why, he was here, there and everywhere, cutting a dash throughout the country districts, though not – as some wryly observed – exactly cutting a swathe through the bushrangers. His sabre had stayed in its scabbard.

The public had been calling for the force to send more officers out to the goldfields, more men to protect the outcome of so much effort by so many diggers. That meant more expenditure, and the one matter both sides of the House could agree upon is that they should resist any increase in expenditure. It was a harsh thing to propose the dismissal of all inspectors as a cost-saving measure, but they had hardly been covering themselves with glory.

What that recommendation was really about was not a consequence of the perceived ineptitude of the police (that is the kind of language used in parliament, impressively grandiose); it was more precisely a resurgence of dissatisfaction with the Police Act, no longer so new. And given that it was associated in particular with its begetter, the Colonial Secretary Charles Cowper, here was an opportunity to attack him. Freddy, whom he had defended again and again, represented all that was wrong with the system. To put it another way, all their collective bungling was identified in him. Quite unfairly, as we have observed, but that is the way public life works.

This was not a good time, then, for Freddy to put in for promotion. His timing always was poor. An additional way of thinking about that, though, is that perhaps he failed to see himself as others saw him. Or perhaps he did not care what others thought about him. Greatness knows itself, as the immortal Bard wrote.[1] And he should know.

Sir Frederick submitted a letter to the department, asking for promotion. Not a rise, a promotion. We do not know just what he had in mind, as his superior was the Inspector-General himself, and that would have amounted to a request to replace him. Which was probably not the wisest course of action, but McLerie was a fair man, and the request was passed on to the Colonial Secretary no less, who returned the request with the remark that Freddy's promotion would be recommended 'whenever he takes Ben Hall'.[2] Take him or leave it.

How, then, had the correspondent of the *Yass Courier* known about this some months earlier – 'Pottinger, who covets a position he can never acquire ...' [see above, p.211].

Yet Ben Hall seemed to have gone missing in action too. That was utterly dispiriting – how could Freddy perform marvels, how could he make sensational arrests when Gardiner and Hall and Gilbert all seemed to have gone to ground? Not that he was one to mope, not while there was a billiard table in the town.

Then out of nowhere – out of Queensland, to be more precise, but at that point in history much the same thing – came the news that everyone had been craving. Frank Gardiner had been arrested. He had been found in Rockhampton, and he was to be extradited to Sydney to stand trial for ... for whatever the police could charge him with. They actually had no one to identify him as involved in the Eugowra escort robbery. A pity they had hung the arrested culprits. Any one of them could have identified Gardiner's role in that grand theft.

Freddy knew who Gardiner was. He had seen him close up, on a moonlit night; he would never forget it. He was not allowed to forget it – every newspaper in the colony kept reminding him. What he needed was someone who had been in on the robbery in the first place, and Freddy knew just who that was. He had never been convinced that John McGuire had clean hands, and perhaps he might be open to persuasion.

For the Inspector was not so stiff-necked as to pass up the chance of winning a conviction. He approached this technically innocent citizen and offered him £300 to give evidence against Gardiner.[3] But McGuire had had rather too much of Sir Frederick's manoeuvres in the past. He had been remanded 14 separate times in 14 consecutive weeks to hold him for the trial that in the end established his innocence.

Anyone could have seen that this latest blandishment would not work. That had nothing to do with the sum on offer. Freddy just didn't get it, that as McGuire wrote it: 'I was not on'. He failed to acknowledge the old saying about honour among thieves. For Freddy, everyone had a price. That is the principle behind reward notices. But if the amount he offered was vaguely reminiscent of a number of pieces of silver, so be it.

Nevertheless, with his nemesis now behind bars, Freddy could afford to present himself to the world as a little more congenial than he had in the past. In April, he presided at a public dinner in Forbes for a departing bank manager, at Vandenberg's estimable Courthouse Hotel. Some 40 gentlemen were reported to have been present.[4] It was considered a thoroughly satisfactory evening, and Freddy's social skills were on full display. That was more like the life he had not wanted to leave behind him. And a whole lot more congenial than camping out under a bush with the frost settling in. An evening for gentlemen, with champagne and cigars. And no place for any regrets about Kate Perry or Mrs Fry.

About the same time that Gardiner arrived back in Sydney under police guard, Ben Hall was heard of again. He had presented himself at the hospital in Cowra with a seriously damaged leg. He was suffering from a centipede bite. Just possibly that was a cover story for something more significant, because there had been a glancing reference to the police inability to catch the 'crippled' bushranger, perhaps in reference to his permanent limp. There had also been reports of him with a bad foot, pointing to something different – whatever the specific cause, he had still been able to outrun, outride, outsmart the police.

Sir Frederick, doubtless, was too preoccupied with the Gardiner case to keep up to date with local press reports. Besides, what glory would there have been in catching his man in a hospital?

As for Gilbert, the rumour was that for several months he had been laid low with an attack of typhoid fever. He had remained hidden for all that time, slung in a hammock beneath an ox wagon, protected from snooping and from any officious questioning.[5] But he was not one to remain in hiding a moment longer than he needed to.

The news that the community at large had been dreading came soon enough. Late in the afternoon at the end of autumn, a trio of horsemen sauntered down the track leading to the Bang Bang Hotel, in what is today known as Koorawatha. It was a convenient halt midway between Cowra and Young. Racehorses were being moved down the road from a previous meeting to the next one, and given that they were such valuable animals, at the owners' request they were protected by a small detachment of troopers. That precaution was well thought of, because the immediate call from the approaching horsemen was that those sitting on the verandah should throw up their hands. The newcomers held carbines and had a variety of pistols in their belts and about their saddles.

They were Ben Hall, Johnny Gilbert, and another evil-looking fellow, known mostly as 'the old man', but known to the police as a former convict, Tom White. He had a string of aliases, just in case. While Hall kept watch over the patrons, Gilbert and White rode around to the back of the hotel to help themselves, as they thought, to the best of the horses. They did not expect to encounter two constables out of uniform – for on this exercise they were on special duty – and they were armed, but with pistols only, not rifles.

Once again there was a prodigious amount of shooting. Bang Bang indeed, though the name apparently is Aboriginal, for that monosyllable appears at the end of quite a number of placenames in that vicinity, and in some Indigenous languages it is associated with death, which in this instance was not inappropriate either. Bullets went whizzing everywhere, the bushrangers firing between 25 and 30 shots; the police were much more deliberate but no more accurate, firing only nine times – who was counting? In the low light, all that swirling smoke and noise was punctuated by choice language from Gilbert: 'take that you — wretch', he bellowed, though perhaps 'wretch' was a genteelism.[6] It is much more likely he remarked on the suspect legitimacy of the officer. All too patently this was not one of those occasions when he presented himself as ladylike.

At some stage, one of the bushrangers took a potshot at the door of the hotel, missing his target there, though the bullet passed through the dress of 'a female who had incautiously exposed herself'.[7] In the light of titillating details like that, the horses were not going to get much of a look in.

All of the press accounts remarked on the self-possession of the racehorses. None of them was scratched, in either sense. The gang was especially interested in the Duke of Athol and Dick Turpin, both of which went on to win significant purses at Randwick in September.

One of the constables kept Gilbert and White at bay, indeed forced them to back away from the stableyard gate. The other rounded the corner of the hotel and surprised Ben Hall, causing him to make a run for it. As he did so, Hall's hat was shot off. The other two galloped off with him, leaving the patrons looking for a drop to calm their nerves no doubt, anxious that the bushrangers might not accept that they had been driven off, anxious that the prize horses which had attracted their interest in the first place were still in the stables. What if they were to come back for them?

Sir Frederick was still at Cowra. His absence has not been explained, for the original plan had been that he too would accompany the horses from Cowra; subsequently he advised the two constabulary heroes that he would follow at a distance. Perhaps he thought an element of surprise was in order. In point of fact, the distance had extended somewhat, and he did not show up until later that night, by which time the hotel had been well and truly barricaded against the return of Ben Hall et al. His lame excuses for not being with the horses when the attack was made failed to convince the Inspector-General.[8] It is not impossible that he had sought the solace of a musical interlude at some homestead along the way.

Not very far at all from Bang Bang was a significant property called Crowther, which clearly represents exasperation with mastering another Aboriginal word, Koorawatha, and meaning possibly 'place of pines', from the predominance of that kind of tree thereabouts. Good country for hiding in, good country for obscuring which direction you are travelling. Given the qualified success of their encounters with Keightley and Campbell, the bushrangers had learned that it could be profitable to kidnap a squatter and hold him for ransom. Curiously – or deliberately – the amount that came to mind whenever they set out on these actions was £300, the same amount with which Sir Frederick had attempted to bait McGuire.

At Crowther, they proposed to take the owner, John Pring. Their timing, though, was nearly as bad as Freddy's. Pring wasn't there.

Pring had connections, especially out in those regions. He had already fended off one such attack on his property, and now with Hall ranging about the district, he appealed for police protection for his family as well as his property. His request to the Inspector-General was turned down, and he felt that he was left with no other choice than to relocate. He found a new sense of security when he moved into a house next door to the Murringo police station.

Pring may not have been where Hall expected to find him; nor had Hall expected Freddy to be right on his tail. Casting around in the vicinity of Pring's station, 'scouring the bush', Sir Frederick with two troopers and a blacktracker – his customary flying squad, and the tracker very likely to have been Billy Dargan, who had by this time established himself as pre-eminently skilful – had picked up hoofmarks and, following them carefully, came to a campsite not at all far from the homestead. Their quarry happened to be standing close to their horses. Hall and his mates were up in their saddles and away in an instant. It was the same old story: 'Sir Frederick and his men gave chase, and fired several shots at the fugitive but without effect. After a chase of two miles the police were distanced as usual.'[9]

Hapless again. But in the days that followed, subsequent reports provided a little more detail. What happened was the other way round. The scouring had been going on for several days, they had been tracking all day, and the men and horses were tired. They were about to make camp, and they had unsaddled their horses when Hall and his accomplices rode up – and beat a retreat as soon as they recognised into whose camp they had stumbled. Pottinger and the police caught their own horses, jumped on to their backs without waiting to saddle up, and galloped off in pursuit. Which might justify why on this particular occasion their pursuit, and their shooting, was ineffective.

It is just as well Freddy was never drafted for the Crimea.

The tracker then led them back along Hall's trail, all the way to his camp on the brow of a bald hill, and from where there was a clear line of sight. Here they found the tent mentioned previously, with a valise in it and stolen cheques and money, later revealed to be to the customary amount, £300.

Once again, Freddy had almost had his man at the end of his barrel; once again he had missed out, and once again he was left with the tatters of what might have been. Here was history repeating itself for a third time. This had gone beyond farce. Freddy was nothing if not consistent – the 'doughty knight' had let Ben Hall slip through his fingers once more. And this was just a few weeks after a rumour had been reported, starting from the *Burrangong Star*, that Sir Frederick was to be appointed Chief Inspector of the Detective Force. If that were to prove true, the correspondents all observed, Freddy would be posted to Sydney.[10] If it had been true, it ceased to be at all likely after this latest shambles.

But as always, it would be unwise to dismiss Freddy as hopelessly incompetent. He was perfectly capable of making plans of his own; or of seizing an opportunity when it offered, providing of course that his gun would go off when it was meant to.

At this time, when reports were popping up of Ben Hall and his companions invading smaller homesteads here and there through the locality, so began another slightly troubling report of a stranger, a bushranger who did not seem to quite know his way around. He had first made his presence known in a gunfight to the south of Forbes, in a paddock at Bundaburra, dodging from tree to tree and firing a good many shots. Because the ground was boggy – those winter rains! – the police horses found the going heavy, and became stuck. Inevitably, he too escaped.[11]

Pottinger may or may not have been involved in that confrontation, for accounts vary, and so does our confidence in them. But he was certainly in the thick of it soon after. He was not about to allow a newcomer to add to his troubles, and it was a worry that this stranger had taken to roaming about between Forbes and the Weddin ranges, the terrain that Gilbert and his gang had made peculiarly their own. Curiously, this fellow was never on a horse, always on foot although he carried a bridle. Possibly that was a mark of optimism. Or possibly there had been a horse but it was stuck in the mud somewhere.

The widely accepted story was that he had come down from Queensland, and was looking to join up with Hall and Gilbert. He was known as the 'Wild Scotchman'.

In a region where there was so much sympathy for Ben Hall and others, and such antagonism towards the police, and to Sir Frederick in particular, it aroused suspicion that this newcomer kept asking questions about the bushrangers of the western district, their movements and their whereabouts. That being the case, he was not given the kind of assistance he was looking for and might have expected. Besides, whoever heard of a bushranger without a horse? They were right to be suspicious.

John McGuire, who had at one time been Ben Hall's partner, and at another time Sir Frederick's dupe, remembered that the Hall trio suspected the Queenslander of being a private detective.[12] They kept him at a distance.

Right at the centre of bushranging activity, on Wheogo station, and about half a mile from the homestead, Sir Frederick, accompanied by a trooper, came across the Scotchman in the bush, and a lot of firing followed. But according to

McGuire: 'it was only Sir Frederick who did the firing, the supposed bushranger did not return it. He got away. The fact is, he was allowed to get away.'[13]

It was a sham, a pretense to convince Hall in particular to connect with the stranger. Clever, but it did not work; nobody was convinced. It was authentic enough – everyone knew Freddy's aim was often astray. And he lost his cap, and had to borrow one from his subordinate so that he would look presentable when he rode back into Forbes.

Bit by bit further details were released. First, it was widely reported that Sir Frederick had wounded the strange bushranger in the arm – the *Sydney Punch* unkindly announced this as a startling intelligence: that Sir Frederick Pottinger had 'fired at a bushranger in a paddock, and hit him'.[14] Then the police released a description, that he was nearly six feet tall, had light hair, no whiskers and moustache, a few light hairs on the tip of his chin and that he was a native of Scotland, wounded in the left forearm, and was supposed to be intent on joining Hall and his gang.[15] That is quite precise in its detail, given that he had been observed no closer than at pistol shot. Though given Freddy's record, that could have been a close encounter. He was now wanted for having fired at Sir Frederick. And it soon became common knowledge that he had come down from Queensland. The absence of any horse remained a mystery.

Later again it became known for the first time that Sir Frederick had also been wounded in the arm at that shootout.[16] In the Treasury and elsewhere such a persistent inflation is known as 'incremental creep'; but we have to allow a more tactical manoeuvre here. It would have done the public no good at the time to learn their hero had been wounded by a mere pedestrian. On the other hand, it did them no harm to learn that their hero was prepared to put himself in harm's way to ensure their safety. A less kindly view might be that he had not been cautious enough.

Sir Frederick informed the police that the 'Scotchman' had shot him in the wrist; but as this information is said to have been supplied to the Queensland police when Pottinger returned to Brisbane – never having been there in the first place, not even to bring Frank Gardiner to trial – then we have to admit that there could be a different kind of manoeuvre altogether; and we should resent the implication that Sir Frederick may in fact have shot himself in the wrist. That quite simply was not the Pottinger way.

Towards the end of September, Ben Hall, together with a bushranger named Dunleavy and 'the old man' from Bang Bang, bailed up a number of people just outside Jugiong – not all at the same time, but whenever they happened to pass by. The bushrangers wanted to keep them out of the way while they awaited either a stagecoach with some wealthy merchants or, on the other hand, the gold escort. Throughout the day they chatted to their captives, and it was soon made clear that the second option was a decoy. They were awaiting that coach full of traders and dealers and bankers.

In the course of their chit-chat they looked for information about the gold escort, but they also revealed a few of their own thoughts upon the way of the world; from our viewpoint the most revealing comment was a passing aside about

Sir Frederick. They were less than impressed by cowardly police officers, but of Freddy they volunteered that he was 'a good deal more fond of women than of fighting bushrangers'.[17] He was a lady's man. That implies that in their view he was no longer a serious menace to them. His time was up as far as they were concerned, just as it was from the point of view of his political masters.

But they also spoke in contempt of Sir Frederick. Hall himself conceded that Freddy had been given had three chances to ping him, and they would make sure he was not given another.

The public at large had likewise formed their own estimation of him. His name was bandied about on all sorts of occasions: for example, a theatre critic reviewing a performance for *Bell's Life* 'noticed, in a neighbouring box, a tall and fashionably dressed man, with an alarming pair of black whiskers, and a stupendous moustache, à la Pottinger, who appeared to me unpleasantly earnest in his ocular admiration of Mrs Wheedler ...'[18] That, incidentally, suggests there may have been something to the story about him ogling young ladies in Hyde Park on the evening he was assaulted. A gallant gentleman indeed.

It would be no use for him to complain about the reporter making free with his name and his character – didn't they know who he was? They knew, or thought they knew, just too well who he was.

As is the way of things, in a calendar year you end where you began. It was time for the holidays, for closure in more respects than parliamentary. The papers began to advertise the acts for the coming Christmas pantomime. Freddy's name was being bandied about there too. He, or a figure taking his part, was to appear in an act introduced by a clown playing a penny trumpet, as the very type of the wrong man in the right place.[19]

The company in which that man could be found.

XIV

THE FINISHING POST

A splendid type of the genuine English gentleman ...

—P.A. SELTH

FOR FREDDY, IT was always about racecourses.

Where the family trajectory resembled the course of a great river, in his case his own had ended up not so much a river as a series of blocked reaches. Lachlan-like, choked with fallen timber; and with more water lying outside the main course than within it.

Here on the vast central western plains, in times of great floods in the district, water found its way down towards another greater water course, though there was no actual junction. In turn that extended by way of an even greater river, all the way through the continent down towards the southern coast, but again without a viable outlet. With no satisfactory course and no satisfactory terminus, the Pottinger model of fame would fail to find a suitable analogy here.

On the other hand, maybe it had.

Freddy's infatuation with racecourses provides another pattern of his existence. A track goes around, and around again, and once more if you wish, until it is time to call a halt. It does not proceed to anywhere. Yet there is a finishing post, when you come to it. The line of his descent had transferred itself to this new allegory, though dim vestiges of the ancestral continuum persisted.

This particular racecourse, Wowingragong, was at the time somewhat unprepossessing. It was nothing like a neatly fenced enclosure, merely a recently cleared area in scrubland, which faded off into infinity.[1] What we have here is nowhere near as inspiriting as the grand allusion to the Nile; but none-theless apt, for all that. This was Freddy, as plain as day.

For the community, the more immediate attraction of the races was in dressing up for the occasion. The motley crew of diggers preened themselves with red silk sashes, the tassels hanging down below their pockets. What a wealth of entertainment was on offer by the dozen or so booths – drink-ing of course, but also dancing on a board floor to the lively jigs of fiddlers, 'having a go at two-up',[2] and trying to pick which thimble was hiding the pea. For younger freckle-faced patrons, there was the excitement of dogs putting a lizard up a tree, where they chucked boondies at it until it descended and raced for another taller tree.

The fixings were none of the best. Saplings marked out the course itself; the winning post might also serve as a pub sign, and the judge's box could be literally that, a gin case for him to stand on. Nobody minded much – the race itself was what mattered. This was a far cry from the elegantly groomed racecourses in England, from Epsom of unhappy memory for example.

Wowingragong racecourse was reassuringly on the extensive flats through which the Lachlan meanders; and it was here that Freddy had arrested Ben Hall three years previously, a move that surprised the community as much as it did Ben Hall himself. That was our Freddy, cleverly unpredictable, always maintaining for himself the element of surprise. Now he was to surprise everyone again.

Throughout his glittering career, we are repeatedly led to understand that Freddy was a splendid horseman, as well as a persistent one. He rode very correctly, English style: straight back, good seat, long stirrups, a lot of bouncing up and down; and his spectacular beard would have been jutting out. You could not mistake him for a bushman. He looked superior, and he presented as superior: he maintained his distinction. He was very aware that he was Sir Frederick Pottinger. Yet there are few opportunities for us to measure just how outstanding a rider he actually was – meaning, we rarely find him in actual competition with others. If he were so accomplished, how was it he could not keep up with fleeing bushrangers?

We have been led to believe too that he knew all about horses, give or take. He ensured that he always had a good horse of his own, a stayer that could carry his significant weight, one on which he could pose to perfection, as at the Young racecourse. He had confidently identified the winner of the Epsom Derby and would have made a fortune if only the track there had been properly measured. And he liked to take in the form of whatever was on display at the sport of kings – and knights of the realm – whether on the turf itself or trackside. The racing game had its pleasures and, just possibly, its temptations too.

Early in the new year of 1865 he undertook something he had not done before, or something he had not admitted to – he entered himself in a race.

That was not what you would expect to see at a race meeting, an inspector of police crouched over his steed and thundering around the track in amongst a lot of other nondescript jockeys. That was hardly the image that the force had of themselves.

But to his way of thinking he had a justification. The police had been encouraged to use their initiative, as well as their judgement, first in taking steps to capture bushrangers. Well, what could be more likely to draw the attention of Hall and Gilbert than to learn that Pottinger was to ride in a race? Freddy, Sir Frederick, would let himself be the honey that would trap them, draw them to the venue, tempt them out into the open.

Apart from the sheer bravado of it, that was pure genius. For this was the part of the world the outlaws liked to call their own – but not for much longer, if he had his way. This was where they liked to think they were most at home. Besides, every man and his dog – and more to the point, his horse – would be there, offering splendid pickings for horse-thieving types. This if anywhere was where they might show themselves. This would be Freddy's finest hour.

It was an ingenious ploy. Early on the first morning of the two-day meeting, Ben Hall and one John Dunn appeared at the camp of a couple of trainers, just 200 yards from the racecourse itself. They stayed there for a couple of hours, detaining everyone who came that way and letting it be known that they were waiting for Sir Frederick to appear at the track. That was rather too long, it seems, for their thirst eventually got the better of them – the weather had been uncommonly hot, and later a thunderstorm would build. Meaning that the track itself would be baked iron-hard; and if rain were to come, it might then turn sticky, as the plains soil is wont to do.[3]

They invited everyone to Tom Higgins's booth, shouted them all to a drink, and Ben Hall accepted a challenge to a race, presumably a footrace (Dunn won it, then someone called Reid came second, and Hall came last; but we should remember his gammy leg). Then the duo went their way, to a chorus of goodwill.

Reports of the carnival affirmed that, of the bushrangers, only Hall and Dunn were present – the New South Wales papers, with one exception, were uniform in this. The intercolonial papers were much more confident that Gilbert was there as well, though not playing such a visible part. The *Yass Courier* in fact asked the question directly: what had become of Gilbert? He had not been seen with the other two, nor was he with them when they helped themselves to some of the racehorses from the venue. He was not, apparently, in their amiable company, wrote the correspondent. And then added, enigmatically, 'Perhaps he is doing the Lothario business amongst the "pretty horsebreakers" of Bland and the Weddin'.[4] Like Freddy, he had built a reputation as a ladies' man.

The exception was the *Burrangong Argus*, from the little township closest to Forbes, and with every likelihood of being written up by an eyewitness. Gilbert was said to have been on or near the course the whole of the time, enjoying the races.

The police did not see him either. Certainly Freddy missed him. Maybe he was in his favoured disguise again.

Hall was at Wowingragong expressly to 'twitch his old acquaintance, Sir Freddy Pott'.[5] He had indeed heard the rumour that Freddy was to ride, though whether on the first day, or the second, or both, was not entirely clear. Whenever it was to be, 'he had a — good mind to shoot him'.[6] The *Burrangong Argus*, whose correspondent would have been present at the race meeting, reported that Freddy rode that very afternoon, on his well-known and provocatively named horse Bushranger,[7] to meet a challenge and take on a bet against a squatter from the local neighbourhood, in a two-horse race. Intriguingly, the other horse was Scrammy Jack – the name of a reasonably well-known bushranger from further north.[8] That was rather egging the bait.

The race was run. It absorbed the attention of the entire crowd, to the extent that not a single spectator reported seeing bushrangers there too. Sadly, Bushranger was left well behind – Scrammy Jack was well ahead by the time the gallant baronet reached the back end of the course, where he might be vulnerable to attack by bushrangers, for that was well away from the largest part of the crowd, who were jostling, as race crowds do, for a view at the finishing post. Freddy was not foolish; or not in this instance. He had made sure that he was accompanied by a number of armed troopers, who rode with him but inside the rail; which rather compromised the element of surprise. By other reports though he had positioned police all around the course, concealed amongst the bushes. Which is presumably where the bushrangers had hidden themselves too.

Some might have thought that Freddy's performance was disappointing, a little flat, like the champagne on offer at the refreshment booths (Freddy most assuredly would have steered clear of the black-bottle beer preferred by the diggers). If he were watching for signs of imminent activity from amongst the shrubbery, then that might explain why he failed to keep up with his competitor. The press was less than sympathetic – they tartly reported 'the policeman's nag, as on more important occasions, being as usual all behind'.[9]

And where in India his father had ridden Bandicoot hard to escape his would-be assassins, Freddy on Bushranger had ridden hard and tried – unsuccessfully – to catch up. Not quite up to scratch, then.

On the other hand, Freddy never contradicted those who said he held back deliberately, so as to entice his prey to emerge from the bushes.

An alternative account, however, of the last race of the first day, and with a more comprehensive field, suggests that a different race, with a bigger field, took place and that in the course of it Sir Frederick was pushed out and out and then quite off the track by a poundkeeper who wanted revenge for police interference in a scam common in his particular line of business. Sir Frederick ended up in amongst the timber, and at quite a disadvantage from the rest of the field – this for the Ladies' Bag, a field of several:

> and when at length he managed to get back again, he was, of course, racing a long way in the rear, and flopping about enough to ruinate any horse's chance ... It was very

> laughable to see Sir Frederick coming home after the other horses were back in the saddling paddock. Both horse and rider were panting.[10]

Everyone was disappointed. Freddy had lost out again, the crowd had not been party to a grand old shoot-out, and Ben Hall did not get to take his pot shot. The rumour, among so many rumours, was that he had expected to see Sir Frederick in racing silks, and as Freddy was in plain clothes, he (Hall) had been deceived. Why he had missed noticing the only rider not in colours, or (depending on which race you thought it was) the only other rider, stretches our incredulity. He was displaying much the same kind of ineptitude, or blindness, as Freddy. Or, more likely, he was still in one of the booths – or reconnoitering his own version of available prizes, tied up under the shade of nearby trees.

But Hall had his justification. Sir Frederick's racing togs were certainly not what he was expecting. In fact Freddy turned up in cord breeches, black riding boots, a black jacket and cap, and carrying a lady's riding whip. Those were, so he claimed, his riding colours in the Old Country.[11] They were not so very different from his police uniform, in fact – indeed, so close for it to have been disconcerting to Ben Hall and his company. Not so different either, come to think of it, from his Eton dress. And with his exuberant beard, for the crowd at large it might have seemed more like the return of the Black Knight.

The press everywhere, in the other colonies too, was astounded that nobody saw the bushrangers, or not that they would admit to. What a joke. Except Freddy just couldn't see it. Not that Ben Hall on this occasion was any better.

The ridicule of Pottinger's attempt to nab Hall and any others of his companions in arms was so universal that his superiors could not have missed it if they had tried. It was everywhere, and for weeks and weeks. This was the worst display of police incompetence yet. This was such an outrageous breach that the department and the government now had to act; though it is also a moot point whether this defiance of regulations conveniently provided the excuse they had been waiting for. Either way, Freddy was to go.

Inspector-General McLerie wrote to Pottinger asking him to explain himself for taking this action, 'it being directly opposed to the regulations of the Department that Officers of the Police should take any part in racing matters'.[12] After his fracas at the billiard table, all officers – and Freddy in particular – had been cautioned about proper and improper behaviour, and preserving respect for the force. It was not acceptable to make a show of oneself.

As he had been asked to explain himself, Freddy could assume he was not in fact dismissed just yet, but suspended. He had to make his case. And he did so, at great length, across 14 foolscap pages.[13] He reiterated that his was a stratagem to lure the bushrangers out into the open; then he went on to argue that it was of great importance for him to be seen as participating in the community, and in this instance an additional factor was that he had not wanted to disappoint the ladies of the district, who were looking forward to him riding for the Ladies' Bag, a prize for which the ladies of the district had busied themselves collecting items. The bag itself was of red, white and blue silk[14] (which would have been a bizarre addition to his accoutrements if he had won the race and had worn the ladies' favour as did the knights of old). It would certainly have been ungracious for him to decline the invitation; it would have been an unsatisfactory reflection on his character and on his social standing.[15] In other words, he was displaying his proper breeding, the behaviour of an English gentleman, if not quite a nobleman.

The obligations were all the greater if it is also correct that he was chairing the race committee at that meeting.[16] He had all sorts of obligations that he did not expect the Inspector-General to appreciate; including, apparently, attending a ball on the evening between the two race days until 4 am, at which time he allowed his men to stand down.[17] There were all those ladies to dance with, to return their favour.

It does not seem at all likely that the race for the Ladies' Bag would have been run exclusively between Freddy and the squatter mounted on his thoroughbred. That private competition must have been a separate race, and run at the end of the second day for a bet. Freddy neglected to admit to that episode, definitely at odds with departmental expectations. And the tone of what he wrote was not deferential. We would not expect that of the dashing baronet. Rather, he was showing that he knew how to do his job.

That was just the point. He had been doing it for years, but public commentary was that he had not. His father though would have been proud of his manoeuvring around the facts of his report. That was the Pottinger way – they told it as it was, forcibly. If from their point of view.

The official correspondence travelled slowly up from the city and down again to headquarters, and Freddy had to await the outcome, because the very real threat of retrenchment was hanging in the air. He was summoned to appear before a panel of enquiry in Sydney. Word of that got out as it always gets out, with or without the bush telegraph. Sir Frederick had his supporters after all, particularly on the diggings. Miners and storekeepers milled together in popular and vocal protest meetings, and a petition with some 300 signatures was sent to the Colonial Secretary.[18]

It did not help that in this interval of voluminous letter-writing and forwarding of official reports, Ben Hall and his accomplice were more active than ever, and more brutally. A constable was shot, an informer stripped and flogged, and with each further criminal act it was remembered that Freddy had missed another opportunity. There was even that mysterious Queenslander still lurking somewhere in the district. In the second half of February he was located, surrounded, arrested and charged with the offence of having shot at Sir Frederick. They found him resting by the bank of a creek near Forbes, quietly reading a book. Too easy.

Freddy wasn't there.

At the beginning of March, Sir Frederick travelled with the Great Western Mail back to Sydney, to apply in person for reinstatement. The horses had laboured to haul the coach up the steep ascent to the heights of the Blue Mountains. At Wascoe's Inn, right at the top of Lapstone Hill, they were taken out of their traces and a new team brought in for the last stage, the long steep descent down to the Cumberland plains. Most of the passengers took the opportunity to ease their bones, stretch their legs, partake of a little refreshment. Freddy had strolled around to the back garden, that ancestral point of departure for Pottingers all those generations ago, where – and here reports again offer a choice of telling detail – he had either picked a bunch of flowers for a pretty young woman inside the coach, or he had stolen some fruit (in quite a few versions, plums. We remember that Freddy was 'adopted' by the plum-popping ambassador, Kiying). It is what you were able to do, being either a baronet, or a high-ranking police officer, or both. Whichever, he was over long about it, and the coach was just starting to trundle off.

Freddy caught up with the coach, and with his free hand swung himself aboard – accidentally knocking a small pistol he had tucked away somewhere inconvenient, maybe in his belt like a bushranger, maybe inside his coat. This road through the mountains was a narrow channel, absolutely prime country for a hold-up. All the wealth of the western plains came down to Sydney through here. So it was advisable to be well armed as well as forearmed.

Yet another account says that he had been 'picking' fruit (cherries, in this instance, close enough to plums if they were of a large variety) for the ladies on board, saw the coach was starting off, ran to vault over the fence and that is when the pistol discharged.[19]

Whatever the case, the gun went off, and Freddy for once had hit a moving target – himself.

In some of the more lurid accounts he could not tell that he had wounded himself because he was covered in plum pulp. Freddy himself was not sure exactly what had happened. Clearly he had made a mess of matters, but he wasn't actually hurting – or not at first. That came later.

Potager/Pottinger: a mess of pottage indeed.

The mail would not wait. Freddy was led into the inn and someone sent for a doctor. Subsequent press reports – there were many such items, for this was exciting news – provided more details. It appears that when the gun went off, he had also been holding a matchbox, presumably to light his inevitable cigar. That would have poisoned the air inside the coach, to the greater discomfort of any other passengers. With his bunch of fruit, it is also a puzzle just how many hands he had.

His pistol was either inside his jacket, or inside his vest (a vest, at the height of summer?) or in his waistcoat. It had fallen out, caught the railing 'and exploded'. Freddy, 'the unfortunate gentleman':

> was at first quite unconscious of being wounded, and immediately inquired if any person had been shot, and it was some little time before he became aware that he had shot himself. Yesterday Sir Frederick was apparently better, but it is stated that the wound which he has accidentally received is of a very dangerous character. The injury, which was at first thought to be inevitably fatal, is now considered as dangerous but doubtful. The course which the bullet took, and the place where it has lodged are uncertain. The medical man first in attendance gave his opinion that the sufferer could not long survive, but two or three other doctors, who have since examined the

> wound, are more sanguine of a favourable termination of the accident. The patient is quite calm and collected, and free from pain, but cannot of course be removed.[20]

That untraceable bullet was to remain elusive. None of the doctors could determine just where it had ended up, other than inside Freddy and probably in his upper abdomen. Sanguine indeed. It was difficult to know just how concerned they should be, as he continued calm and collected, and free from pain.

There were, of course, alternative scenarios. One persistent notion was that he had attempted to commit suicide. Was there something about the young Pottingers that encouraged such a suspicion? For exactly the same rumour had circulated at the death of his cousin Eldred in Hong Kong.

Another was that Freddy was showing off to young ladies in the coach and the pistol went off accidentally. The New South Wales police appear to subscribe to this possibility.[21] The Pottinger family historian has Freddy the single passenger inside the coach, and as it travelled down the slope towards Sydney and Freddy's approaching interview, the driver heard a shot, stopped the coach and found Freddy slumped on the seat.[22] If Freddy had intended to shoot himself, then he had made a fine mess of that too. He was not to be trusted with guns. A billiard cue was more his weapon of choice.

Whatever the case, the end result was that he was now in a bad way. The likeliest sequence after that is that he rested for several days before being sent down from Wascoe's to his club in Sydney, where he was instructed to take to his bed – but first, the obnoxious bullet had to be located and removed, and Freddy stitched up. As the days went on, he appeared to be recuperating quite well, then signs of a temperature and a fever manifested themselves, and he began to sink.

Or (it will be no surprise that yet another scenario was set out), while he lay recovering in the hotel, friends of his were playing cards, and Freddy could not contain himself. He rose from his sick bed and went to watch the game. That brought on the relapse, and he was taken to Sydney for more urgent treatment.

Lying in the half-darkness of the shuttered room at his club, he could hear the clip-clop of horses and the rattle of carriage wheels on the cobblestones outside. The weeks went by, and the hoped-for recovery was thwarted. Inflammation had set in. Someone came in to tell him that James McPherson, the 'Wild Scotchman', had been caught at Billabong Creek near Forbes and was now in Sydney awaiting trial for shooting at him. Freddy would have to appear as witness, indeed the only witness. Without him there to identify the perpetrator, the case would collapse.

That was not of enough interest to make him rally. He had had quite enough of bushrangers. He didn't want to see any more.

He hadn't seen them in the first place.

It turned out that Freddy had not timed matters very well. As many observed, he used to live beyond his means. He borrowed money and ran up accounts everywhere, paying off his obligations whenever he received a remittance from home.[23] At the time of his accident, so it emerged, he was in debt to the amount of £60, and there was a further claim against him of almost £160, close to $9000 today. When the bank manager who was appointed to wind up his affairs wrote to Sir Frederick's brother William (who therefore inherited the baronetcy), the reply came swiftly enough, that the family was not responsible for Freddy's debts. *Virtus in ardua* again, with a new twist. How very Pottingeresque.

He sank further and further into his bed, drifting in and out of consciousness. From time to time someone would come in and wipe his extensive brow with a cool cloth. Someone came to draw the curtains. And he, just lying there, staring, inert, unaware.

Someone came in and closed his eyes, his unseeing eyes.

* * *

The funeral notice appeared, and friends of 'this unfortunate gentleman' were invited to attend. The funeral cortege – the hearse of course, three mourning coaches and the coaches of several leading citizens – started out from the Victoria Club in Castlereagh Street and made its way out to Randwick, to St Jude's Anglican Church. St Jude, patron saint of desperate cases and lost causes. What a joke. Freddy didn't get to see that one either.

He did have a last laugh though. He was buried about as close to the finishing post at Randwick as it was possible to get. His finishing post, his gravestone, was a broken column. Conventionally, that denotes a life cut short. In his case it was one he was never able to complete. He had been beaten to the post more than once throughout his life.

Besides, if he couldn't see what was in front of his face, why on earth had he ever expected to get anywhere?

Blind Freddy.

DÉJÀ VU

'... all great men are frauds.'

—BONAR LAW, in LORD BEAVERBROOK
Politicians and The War

THE BLOODY FIELD OF WHEOGO.

'It was a glorious victory!'—SOUTHEY[1]

THE moon rides high in a starry sky, and, through the midnight
gloom,
A faery scene of woodland green her silver rays illume;
Dark mountains show a ridge of snow against the deep blue sky,
And a winding stream with sparkling gleam flows merrily
murmuring by.

Not a sound is heard, save the bough when stirr'd by the night
wind's moaning sigh,
Or, piercing and shrill, echo'd back by the hill, the curlew's
mournful cry:
And twinkling bright in the shadowy night a distant taper shines,
And seated there is a wanton fair that in amorous sadness pines.

For her lord is gone, and she sits alone, alone in a desolate home,
But it was not her lord that she then deplor'd, for she loved to see
him roam;
The joy of her heart is a Ranger smart, who, lion-like, roves in
the night,
And with supper all spread, and a four-post bed, she waits by the
flickering light.

Equipp'd for fight, in trappings bright, came a band of warriors
there,
By gallant Sir Fred, right gallantly led, the Ranger to seize in a snare.
They spread o'er the ground, and the house they surround,
nine men with revolver and gun,
'A reward's on his head', cried the gallant Sir Fred, 'and we're nine
to the Bushranger's one!'

Still gleam'd the light through the shades of night, and still the
pale moon shone,
But no Ranger came to cheer the dame as she sat by the light alone;
The warriors bold were freezing with cold, and thought it was time
to start,
When the echoing beat of a horse's feet sent the blood in a rush,
to the heart!

At gentle speed, on snow-white steed, and singing a joyous song,
To the twinkling light in the shadowy night the Ranger rides
along;
A stalwart man was he to scan, and flush'd with ruffian pride,
For in many a fray he had won the day, and the New Police defied!

Up started then Sir Fred. and his men, with cock'd carbine in hand,
And call'd aloud on the Ranger proud, on pain of death, to 'stand!'
But the Ranger proud, he laughed aloud, and bounding rode away,
While Sir Frederick Pott, shut his eyes for a shot, and miss'd – in
his usual way.

His warriors then, like valiant men, with their carbines blazed away,
The whistling lead on its mission sped, but whither none can say;
For the snow white steed, at gentle speed, bore the Ranger from
their view,
And left Sir Fred, to return to bed, – there was nothing else to do.

But Sir Frederick Pott, with rage was hot, as he looked at his
warriors eight,
Eight to one, with revolver and gun! and he cursed his luckless fate;
For he shudder'd to think how his glory would sink when the
country heard of the mess,
And the tale was told of his warriors bold in the columns of the
Press.

In fury then he marched his men where dwelt the wanton fair,
With warlike din they all enter'd in, and search'd and ransack'd
there.
In slumber sound, a boy they found, whereon Sir Frederick said,
'By a flash in the pan we missed the man, so we'll take the boy
instead!'

SNOWY RIVER.

August 18.

THE FEARCE AND BLUDDY BATTLE OF THE WEDDEN MOUNTINS.

DONE INTO RIME BY DAMPHOOL, JUNR.[2]

I.

Nine valyent men of New South Wales, all armed to the teeth,
Went forth to take won Gardiner, of Bushrangers the chefe;
And then Sur Frederick, he did say, 'ure rein will now be brefe;
For all the fearful deads 'uve done, 'ure neck will come to grefe!
Ho, yes he sed, fierce Gardiner, 'ure neck will come to grefe.

II.

Sur Frederick then, and his nine men, set hout wun winter nite
Towards the Wedden Mountins, as the moon was shinin brite,
And how the jackasses did larf upon the branches hite,
To see nine valyent caveliers they thort a goodly site!
And all to take wun Gardiner they thort a goodly sight.

III.

'Twas sed in town wun Missus Brown had got a hous of corl,
A little snug and quiet spot beneth a gum tree torl—
A stabel for his prancing gray behind the cottage worl,
And for himself a supper nice, the cosey bed and orl—
It plesent is, quoth Gardiner, the cosey BED and orl.

IV.

Now of Sur Frederick's fighting men, too stood behind the pump,
And three bob'd down their valyent heds just hidden by a stump,
The others where placed in the rear to hit is horse's rump,

And then bold Pottinger did say his life's not worth a dump,
So thort the laughing jackasses, his life's not worth a dump.

V.

And sune hup rode bold Gardiner upon is prancing gray,
And then hup jumped bold Pottinger, and sed my frend
good day,
Hive got nine valyent men at arms yourself to take away,
And too the gallus we will bare you, gallus bird, away!
Ho, will you so, ses Gardiner, I wish you then good day.

VI.

As Gardiner was trotting of, Sur Frederick took his gun,
And stil he thort that Gardiner was poking of his fun;
From him and is nine valyent men, to think that he could run;
So taking ame, at Gardiner he sed my frend ure dun,
And all the larfing jackasses they thort that he was dun.

VII.

And then instead of a report there only wos a snik:
Sed he, hoo loded that ere gun did do a skurvy trik—
But hat the sight of Gardiner the valyent men turned sik,
While Gardiner he larfed aloud, and rode of like a brik,
And orl the larfing jackasses they sed he was a brik.

VIII.

Sur Frederick then harranged is men, and sed each skurvey nave
Shall ave the sak when he got back hoo could so bad behave;
So very careful was they orl, their preshus soles to save,

And then they took a little boy, they wos so very brave,
Not wun that day did run away! they wos so werry brave!

IX.

The milartry are hordered hout, and trupers too, 'tis sed,
Commanded by wun Hamiltun, Sur Frederick insted;
Tremenjus Black will show the trak hoo fills us orl with dred;
And each for Gardiner's char-med life will cary char-med led,
Cast at the solemn midnite hour wen good fokes are abed.

LAYS BY SIR POT AND JAR.[3]

I. – O, THIS IS NO' FRANK GARDINEER.

O, this is no Frank Gardineer,
And not a tithe sae fierce as he.
O, weel ken I Frank Gardineer;
He has got sic a doun on me.

Frank Gardineer's form, Frank Gardineer's face,
Has aften brought me to disgrace,
An' made me run a fearfu' race,
Lest be should lay his hands on me.
O, this is no', &c.

A monstrous loon, sae fierce and tall,
He lang has held these roads in thrall;

An' aye it chills my vera saul,
    For fear he'd catch a glimpse o' me.
O, this is no', &c.

A thief sae plucky's Gardineer;
    I tremble every sound I hear,
Lest I should see him standing near
    Wi' pistol cock'd, and aim'd at me.
O, this is no', &c.

He has escap'd from Saunderson;
    And Battye, too, has found him gone;
His tracks I'll never hit upon –
    For that you may depend on me.
O, this is no', &c.

NOTE. – The reader of Burns cannot fail to see how closely I have kept to his beautiful ballad, 'O, this is no' my ain lassie.' – Sir P. and J.

II. – WHY BIDE YE IN YOUR BED, MY CHIEF?

Why bide ye in your bed, my chief –
    Why bide ye in your bed?
Frank Gardiner is once more abroad,
    An' swears he'll punch your head;
He'll punch your head for you, my chief;
    As punch'd it ne'er has been

But aye he loot the tears down fa'
    For fear he suld be seen.

O, now's the time to courage show,
    Nor let that cheek grow pale,
Young Frank, the chief of Wheogo,
    He vows your lugs he'll nail –
Aye, nail them to his cabin door,
    In sight o' his bush queen;
But aye he loot the tears down fa'
    For fear he suld be seen.

Frank Gardiner was upon the road –
    All knew that he was there;
They went unto the chief's abode,
    To see if he were there.
They found him not, in bower nor ha',
    But 'neath the bed I ween,
Wi' sheet and blanket covered o'er,
    For fear be suld be seen.

NOTE. – My Scottish readers will perceive that the above is an attempt to popularise in the wild bush of Australia the beautiful music of Jock o' Hazeldean. – Sir P. and J.

THERE'S WHISKEY IN THE JAR[4]

As I was a-crossin' over the Abercrombie Mountains,
I met Sir Frederick Pottinger, and his money he was countin'.
I then produced my pistols to acquaint him of his danger,
Sayin' 'Stand and deliver for I am a bold bushranger'.

[CHORUS]
With a ma shar-ring-ah-da
Ri too ra laddy oh, Ri too ra laddy oh,
There's whiskey in the jar.

Now it's early in the morning about six o'clock or seven,
There's troopers all around me in numbers odd and even,
Y'see Jenny had got me chargers and she dampened them with
  water
Oh the devil take her mother, for rearin' such a daughter.

[CHORUS]

So they sent me off to Bathurst Gaol without no judge or writin'
For the robbin' of Sir Fred on the Abercrombie Mountain,
But they didn't take my fist from me and I knocked out all the
  sentries!
So I bid fond farewell to Sir Fred and all his Gentry!

[CHORUS]

ENDNOTES

THE SADDLING PADDOCK

1 Sidney A. Baker, *The Australia Language*, Angus and Robertson, Sydney, 1945, p. 269.

2 *The Referee: A journal of sport, pastime and the stage* (Sydney), 12 April 1911.

I. THE POTTINGER FOUNDATION

1 Henry Fielding, *The History of the Life of the Late Mr Jonathan Wild the Great*, London, 1743, Book 1, ch. II.

2 That caused difficulties subsequently. The sovereign was thought to have shown Jacobite sympathies when William of Orange came over the horizon. That might have been justified as a means of minimising local disorder, or it might have been a tactical mistake. The Pottingers would have a history of crossing borders, and indeed of drawing up new ones; see Raymond Gillespie, *Early Belfast: The origins and growth of an Ulster town to 1750* (Belfast Natural History and Philosophical Society in association with the Ulster Historical Foundation, Belfast 2007), p. 120.

3 See 'List of the sovereigns and burgesses of Belfast', *Belfast Monthly Magazine*, 4, 1810, pp. 176–80. The title 'Sovereign' was restyled 'Mayor' in 1842.

4 See George Pottinger, *Sir Henry Pottinger: First governor of Hong Kong*, Sutton Publishing, Stroud, Eng., 1997, p. 3.

5 Gillespie, *Early Belfast*, p. 147. The construction of these little alleys took place in the early eighteenth century.

6 This claim was made in the *Philadelphia Inquirer* in 1897.

7 George Pottinger, *Sir Henry Pottinger*, p. 2.

8 'Sir John Burke ... had few editorial scruples, and many fanciful medieval anecdotes were presented as fact. After his death in 1892, subsequent editors attempted to rebuild the reputation of *Burke's Peerage* ...'; see 'Errors in *Burke's Peerage – Encyclopedia Britannica*', https://www.britannica.com/topic/Burkes-Peerage.

9 George Pottinger, *Sir Henry Pottinger*, p. 2.

10 Thus from George Pottinger, *Sir Henry Pottinger*, p. 3. It is a struggle to preserve one's enthusiasm about all these unimaginatively named Pottingers. Fortunately, they are not our prime concern in these pages.

11 John Bancks, *The History of the Life and Reign of William III*, Charles Marsh and Thomas Davies, London, 1744, p. 278. Edward missed the Battle of the Boyne, and likewise the Glencoe massacre, which followed a year or two later. Glencoe is just up a loch across the Sound from the Island of Mull. That misspelling may have been the typesetter's mistake, rather than Bancks's.

12 Stephen Leacock, *Nonsense Novels* (1911), a professor of political economy, and therefore obviously qualified to give a reliable account of just about anything, of course!

13 See William Dalrymple, *The Anarchy: The relentless rise of the East India Company* (Bloomsbury, London, 2019): 'One of the very first Indian words to enter the English language was the Hindustani slang for plunder: loot. According to the *English Oxford Dictionary*, this word was rarely heard outside the plains of north India until the late eighteenth century, when it suddenly became a common term across Britain. To understand how and why it took root and flourished in so distant a landscape, one need only visit Powis Castle in the Welsh Marches' (p. xxiii).

14 George Pottinger, *Sir Henry Pottinger*, p. 4.

15 Eldred Pottinger Esq. of Craigavade is later listed among the original members of the Northern Whig Club, April 1790. So is his father-in-law, John Crawford Gordon, of Florida (House). So is his subsequent competitor, the Hon. R. Stewart of Mount Stewart, whose title Viscount Castlereagh was not conceded until 1796.

16 George Pottinger, *Sir Henry Pottinger*, p. 3.

17 ibid., p. 4.

18 Henry Joy, *Historical Collections relative to the Town of Belfast: from the earliest period to the Union with Great Britain*, George Berwick, Belfast, 1817, p. 433; see also Charles Teeling, *Personal Narrative of the Irish Rebellion of 1796*, Washbourne, London, 1828, p. 85.

19 George Pottinger, *Sir Henry Pottinger*, p. 2.

20 Mary Lowry, *The Story of Belfast and its Surroundings*, Headley Brothers, London, 1913 (repr. Appletree Press, Belfast, 2009), pp. 57–8. Indeed, we do not. Ms Lowry was concerned at what, if any, punishment was meted out. The boys were beaten, then expelled. Henry Pottinger would have been aged only three when that untoward event is said to have taken place; or two years deceased, for it actually took place in 1867. Irish blarney?

21 Maud Diver, *The Hero of Herat: A frontier biography in romantic form*, Constable & Co., London, 1914, p. 13.

22 ibid.

23 John Burke, *Genealogical and Heraldic History of the Commoners of Great Britain and Ireland*, vol. IV, Henry Colburn, London, 1838, p. 442.

24 See National Archives of Ireland, Records of the Chief Secretary of Ireland, March 1819, ref. CSO/RP/1819/ 696. Thomas Pottinger's address at that time is in Lower Gardiner St, Belfast, not the insistently asserted Mountpottinger residence.

25 George Pottinger, *Sir Henry Pottinger*, pp. 5–6.

26 ibid., p. 7.

27 William Broadfoot, 'Sir Henry Pottinger' (rev. James Lunt), *Oxford Dictionary of National Biography*, Oxford, 2004.

II. THE NEW DIASPORA

1 Bombay (from Portuguese 'Bom Bahia') had long been known as Mumbai in the original language, Marathi. That name was reclaimed in 1995.

2 *The Letters of Rudyard Kipling 1911–19* (vol. IV), ed. Thomas Pinney, University of Iowa Press, Iowa City, 1999, p. 233, n. 2.

3 George Pottinger, *Sir Henry Pottinger*, p. 8.

4 For a concise survey of this tolerance see Craig Murray, *Sikunder Burnes: Master of the Great Game*, Birlinn, Edinburgh, 2016, pp. 20–2.

5 *The Watchman* (London), 15 January 1845.

6 Henry Pottinger, *Travels in Beloochistan and Sinde: Accompanied by a geographical and historical account of those countries, with a map*, Longman, Hurst, Rees, Orme and Brown, London, 1816, p. 365. Admittedly, his remarks come at the end of his book in 1816, that is eight years after the event, when he was just 19. That is still rather early in his career. His conviction about British dignity would be comical if it were not so offensive.

7 ibid., p. 376.

8 ibid., p. 377.

III. JUST DESERTS

1 John Ure, *Sabres on the Steppes: Danger, diplomacy and adventure in the Great Game*, Constable, London, 2012, p. 2.

2 George Pottinger, *Sir Henry Pottinger*, p. 10.

3 ibid., p. 63.

4 ibid., p. 43.

5 ibid., p. 65.

6 ibid., p. 101.

7 ibid., p. 145.

8 ibid., p. 198.

9 ibid., p. 235.

10 John Ure, *Shooting Leave: Spying out Central Asia in the Great Game*, Constable, London 2010, p. 19.

IV. THE SPYMASTER

1 See *Dublin University Magazine*, vol. 28, October 1846, p. 432, and Sir Henry's correction in a letter to the editor, vol. 28, December 1846, p. 768. A footnote to the original article adds a revealing detail: 'The horse which, by his speed, thus saved his master's life, was then eight years old. He lived to the year 1834, and carried his owner – no light weight – up to nearly that period.'

2 George Pottinger, *Sir Henry Pottinger*, p. 30.

3 Roger Houghton, *A People's History 1793–1844 from the Newspapers: Asia 1820–1844 (part 4)*: Saturday, 16 September 1820. 'Married 9th September 1820 at St Thomas' Church Bombay by the Reverend T. Carr, Capt Henry Pottinger, Collector at Ahmednugger, and Susanna Maria, eldest daughter of the late Capt Cooke of H M's 2nd Regiment' (houghton.hk).

4 Murray, *Sikunder Burnes*, p. 19; he is drawing upon William Dalrymple's *White Mughals* (Harper Collins, London, 2002).

5 Anne de Courcy, *The Fishing Fleet: Husband-hunting in the Raj*, Phoenix Paperback, London, 2012, 2013, p. 232.

6 Cookesborough was also the name of the Cooke family seat. It was finally the residence of one of the strangest figures of Westmeath county history, a famous eccentric, Adolphus Cooke. He had a curious resemblance to Spike Milligan, not only in looks but in his asserted views. His narrative is not summarised here as it would put the story of the Pottingers at too much of a disadvantage.

7 'Sir Henry's lady is a remarkably fine-looking woman', *The Watchman*, 15 January 1845.

8 Anne de Courcy recounts the continuation of that activity into the post-Company days, but the circumstances are comparable: 'Getting engaged in the Raj was a bit like speed dating' (de Courcy, *The Fishing Fleet*, p. 202).

9 Ahmednagar became a place of some renown only later, when Spike Milligan was born there. Given the Milligans washed up in downtown Woy Woy, NSW, one is tempted to speculate whether there is some kind of shadow between the stories of the two families.

10 George Pottinger, *Sir Henry Pottinger*, p. 38, n. 16.

11 ibid., pp. 31–2.

12 It was evidently a substantial building. 'Pottinger's residence stood until the earthquake of 2002; it was from 1946 used as the Indian Army's Officers' Mess' (Murray, *Sikunder Burnes*, p. 35). The fort too was severely damaged, and the walls about the old town came tumbling down.

13 Murray, *Sikunder Burnes*, p. 27.

14 George Pottinger, *Sir Henry Pottinger*, p. 162. The two young women

went through the customary torments. One died at Poona within three months, the other managed a marriage from Uncle Henry's residence in Bhuj and died a year or so later, having accomplished little more than falling out with her aunt. You have to wonder whether it had been worthwhile. One of them, discontented with her aunt's supervision of them, and more especially with her inability to keep a confidence, wrote: 'anything you say before her is repeated to anyone who chooses to listen to it. Do not think I would say so ill-naturedly even though I have often experienced how little is to be trusted to her veracity.'

V. THE SORCERER'S APPRENTICE

1 See George Pottinger, *The Afghan Connection: Adventures of Major Pottinger* (Scottish Academic Press, 1983, p. 7): Eldred 'was a great boxer, and was frequently distinguished in pugilistic encounters with the toughs of Croydon'. He draws upon H.M.V. Bart, *Addiscombe: its heroes and men of note*, 1894.

2 Quoted in Rodney Atwood, *The Life of Field Marshal Lord Roberts*, Bloomsbury Publishing, London, 2014, p. 19. Bourne noted the cold dark dormitories too, the less than intense commitment to teaching, and decided in the end that Addiscombe was not, properly speaking, a military academy.

3 Diver, *The Hero of Herat*, p. 14.

4 ibid.

5 George Pottinger, *Sir Henry Pottinger*, p. 7.

6 Quoted in George Pottinger, *Sir Henry Pottinger*, p. 6. He identifies the Poona Auxiliary Horse, 1835, and the Kutch Irregular Horse, 1836. These would also seem to provide an invitation to the likes of Edward Lear; or possibly Gilbert and Sullivan.

7 Cited in Murray, *Sikunder Burnes*, p. 162.

8 ibid., p. 262.

9 ibid., p. 160.

10 Thomas Pottinger to John Cam Hobhouse, February 1839, quoted in Murray, *Sikunder Burnes*, p. 265.

11 A copy of a document from the India Records Office in the British Library shows what he had left behind when he made his escape. He

(and then his brother John, on his behalf) petitioned for compensation for the loss of personal effects, including an extensive library not just of geology and politics and history, but also of poetry (Chaucer, Wordsworth, Shelley, Byron), Burke on the *Sublime and the Beautiful* and the very popular and satirical Canadian/American book, Thomas Haliburton's *The Clockmaker: or The sayings and doings of Sam Slick*. There was scientific equipment, there were guns and swords, clothing – both European and Persian – carpets, wine and spirits, and six horses. The application was for over £2000, or something of the order of £70,000 today. See https://blogs.bl.uk/untoldlives/2014/07/pottingers-property-lost-in-afhghanistan.html. Eldred Pottinger was in command of a small garrison of Ghurkas at Kohistan, north of Kabul; see William Dalrymple, *Return of a King*, Bloomsbury, London, 2013, p. 263.

12 Recounted in detail in Murray, *Sikunder Burnes*, pp. 364–73. By report the Afghans were offended not so much by the presence of Burnes's retinue of attractive Kashmiri girls as that he used to bathe with his Afghan mistress 'in the hot water of lust and pleasure, as the two rubbed each other down with flannels of giddy joy and the talc of intimacy. Two memsahibs, also his lovers, would join them' (cited in Dalrymple, *Return of a King*, p. 201). Presumably the astonishment was not in the remarkable fact of bathing. The tipping point, though, appears to have been that a runaway slave girl was discovered in bed with him. For what it is worth, even George MacDonald Fraser's Flashman dismisses Burnes as 'that conceited Scotch buffoon' (*Flashman*, Penguin, Harmondsworth, 1969, p. 74) – but then Burnes and Flashman were in private matters something of an uncomfortable pigeon pair. It is of milder interest that the word 'rundi', a Hindi word meaning a dancing girl or prostitute, might be the root of the English word 'randy'; see Dalrymple, *Return of a King*, p. 501.

VI. A PUFF OF SMOKE

1 Murray, *Sikunder Burnes*, p. 260.

2 ibid., p. 39: 'In 1828, the monopoly on sales of opium from British India accounted for 16 per cent of the EIC's revenue. Opium sales to China through agents (it was against Chinese law) paid for the vast amounts

of tea the Company exported from China to the UK ... The trade was so valuable the Company gave its opium agents the colossal pay of £7500 p.a. – more than the Chancellor of the Exchequer, the highest British government salary.'

3 Sir William Watson, 'A study in contrasts', in *The Collected Poems of William Watson*, John Lane, London, 1899, vol. 1, pt 1, ll 42–3.

4 'The Iron-headed Old Rat, the sly and cunning ring-leader of the opium smugglers has left for the Land of Mist, of fear from the Middle Kingdom's wrath', Priscilla Napier, *Barbarian Eye: Lord Napier in China*, Brassey's, London, 1995.

5 Frank Welsh, *A Borrowed Place: The history of Hong Kong*, Harper Collins, London, 1994, pp. 146–7.

6 G.B. Endacott, *A Biographical Sketch-book of Early Hong Kong*, Hong Kong University Press, Hong Kong, 1962, 2005, pp. xiv–xv. Elliot was notified of his recall on 29 July 1841; see George Pottinger, *Sir Henry Pottinger*, p. 70.

7 See 'China and the Chinese', *Dublin University Magazine*, vol. 32, July 1848, p. 40. The anonymous memoir was written in 1846.

8 See 'Sir Henry Pottinger, Bart', *Dublin University Magazine*, vol. 28, October 1846, p. 438. This was the estimation of one of the delegation.

9 George Pottinger, *Sir Henry Pottinger*, p. 101.

10 Difficult, but not impossible: it was robbed on 26 March 1843; see Sheilah Hamilton, *Watching over Hong Kong: Private policing 1841–1941*, Hong Kong University Press, Hong Kong, 2008.

11 Yeewan Koon, 'The face of diplomacy in nineteenth-century China', in Kendall Johnson (ed.), *Narratives of Free Trade: The commercial cultures of early US–China Relations*, Hong Kong University Press, Hong Kong, 2012, p. 139.

12 *Illustrated London News*, 1843.

13 Frank Welsh, *A Borrowed Place*, p. 147.

14 Susanna Hoe, *The Private Life of Old Hong Kong: Western women in the British colony 1841–1941*, Oxford University Press, Hong Kong, 1991, p. 58. The source of this description is from a naval surgeon, Edward Cree, who encountered her at Henry Pottinger's residence.

15 Ernst Eitel, *Europe in China*, Kelly & Walsh, London, 1895, p. 188.

16 Murray, *Sikunder Burnes*, p. 38.

17 Murray, https://www.craigmurray.org.uk/archives/2017/09/the-appalling-pottingers/.

18 Hoe, *The Private Life of Old Hong Kong*, p. 60. The name Henry Morgan would have had unfortunate historical associations.

19 ibid., p. 59.

20 George Pottinger, *Sir Henry Pottinger*, p. 126.

VII. THE SWIRLING CAPE

1 John Norris, *The First Afghan War 1838–42*, Cambridge University Press, Cambridge, 1967, p. 43.

2 George Pottinger, *Sir Henry Pottinger*, pp. 134–5.

3 Memorial from Lieutenant John Pottinger of the Regiment of Artillery respecting certain claims of his late brother, Major Eldred Pottinger, for allowances and compensation alleged to be due to him for loss of his property in Afghanistan, October 1842 to June 1844 [IOR/F/4/2058/94289]. The Governor-General determined that he was entitled only to compensation for what he might have lost on military rather than political service, and that compensation had no relation to the value of the property lost.

4 'Sir Henry Pottinger, Bart', *Dublin University Magazine*, vol. 28, October 1846, p. 442.

5 ibid., p. 432.

6 Christopher Hussey, *Eton College, with an Account of Oppidan Eton*, Country Life, London, 1922, 1952, p. 13.

7 Senior students, and the more privileged Collegians, had their own room; and day boys, Oppidans, took comfortable lodgings in the village.

8 *Grahamstown Journal*, 6 February 1847.

9 *Advertiser and Mail* (Cape Town), 28 April 1866, letter signed 'Tancred'; cited in George Pottinger, *Sir Henry Pottinger*, p. 150.

10 Frank Welsh, *South Africa: A narrative history*, Kodansha America Inc., New York, 1999, p. 189.

11 George McCall Theal, *History of South Africa from 1795 to 1872*, vol. 3, Swann Sonnenschein, London, 1908, p. 307.

12 George Pottinger, *Sir Henry Pottinger*, pp. 143–4.

13 Theal, *History of South Africa*, pp. 309–10.

VIII. FORTUNE'S WEAL

1 P.A. Selth, 'A splendid type of the genuine English gentleman: Sir Frederick William Pottinger, Bart, 1831–1865', *Canberra Historical Journal*, March 1974, p. 21.

2 George Pottinger, *Sir Henry Pottinger*, p. 153.

3 ibid.

4 Lord Wilson was notably unsympathetic, even to the point of hostility, in an untitled review in *Pacific Affairs* (vol. 71, no. 2, Summer 1998, pp. 246–7), where he writes that 'Sir Henry Pottinger in Madras appeared very indolent – a character, it may be added, which he had previously borne at the Cape ... Incompetent ...'

5 Mick Jagger wore one on TV in 1966, bought on Kings Road – apparently he quite understood the attraction.

6 Selth, 'A splendid type of the genuine English gentleman', p. 21.

7 'Attorney-General v Sir Frederick Pottinger', Court of Exchequer, 24 April 1861, *Law Journal Reports* vol. 30, pt 2, pp. 287, 291. This is in summary of Sir Frederick's submission, and we cannot but admire the aplomb with which he adroitly sidesteps exactly what that unpleasantness was, given his own central role in it.

8 Frank Welsh, *A Borrowed Place*, p. 156.

9 *Illustrated London News*, 14 February 1856, p. 129.

10 The proceedings were printed in newspapers across the country; see, for example, the *Morning Chronicle*, 11 August 1857; *Reynolds Newspaper*, 16 August 1857. Much of the proceedings are also accessible through Mark Matthews's website, *Traps: The Complete and Authentic Life and Times of Australian Bushranger Ben Hall and his Associates*, though with some unfortunate chortling at the lurid aspects. He should have remembered that Sir Frederick was a dignified member of a dignified family.

11 George Pottinger, *Sir Henry Pottinger*, p. 163.

12 Selth, 'A splendid type of the genuine English gentleman', p. 21. His were substantial winnings too, of £500, which converts to something in the order of £17,000 today.

IX. A TOUCH OF ENGLISH

1 *Henry V*, Part I, act 1, lines 28–29. With Miss Perry's given name, kiss me Kate indeed.

2 See 'List of unclaimed letters for the month of March', *New South Wales Government Gazette* (Sydney), 13 April 1860, p. 172.

3 *Goulburn Chronicle* (10 November 1860, p. 2), was delighted at his presence in the community, for he had 'on several occasions furnished contributions to the columns of this journal, displaying a refined taste and lively fancy. His literary habits we trust will, under more favourable circumstances, be confirmed ...'

4 *Bathurst Free Press*, 5 May 1860, p. 3.

5 *Sydney Morning Herald*, 28 June 1861, p. 8.

6 'Very strange tales,/Are told of gentlemen in New South Wales' (John Dunmore Lang, *An Historical & Statistical Account of New South Wales*, London, 1852, vol. I, p. 137).

7 'Reminiscences of Dan Mayne', *Forbes Times*, 31 July 1907, cited in *Remember When: Stories and memories of Forbes and District*, Forbes Family History Group, Forbes, nd, p. 23.

8 The Forbes correspondent supplied copy to the *Monaro Mercury*, 9 January 1863, p. 5.

9 See *Sydney Morning Herald*, 7 June 1864, p. 2. Some years later the *Forbes Advocate* (23 September 1921, p. 9), identifies her instead as Miss Coyle, 'a tall, strapping woman, very "horsey", and was bred the right way; she was a lovely horsewoman ... and knew all there was to be known about racehorses'. She was upset about the finish of a Boxing Day race in which she had a horse entered, as were the crowd. Sir Frederick and his troopers arrived, handcuffed some of the rioters, but she laid into him with her whip, 'dealing with him rather severely'.

10 The report of the trial was copied by numerous newspapers at the time, usually with a leading remark that the affair appears to have been highly discreditable to both parties; originally in the *Yass Courier*, 26 February 1861, p. 2.

11 See 'Gambling', *Maitland Mercury*, 29 March 1862, p. 2. The editorial makes the point that Sir Frederick's bad luck was not in the gambling, but in being made notorious because of it. Touché.

12 *Illawarra Mercury*, reprinted from the *Lachlan Observer*, 18 March 1862, p. 4.

13 In point of fact he was born at Boro Creek, south of Goulburn, an illegitimate child, and he ran away from home at the age of 10. That suggests its own challenge to a comprehensive education; see D.J. Shiel, *Ben Hall, Bushranger* (University of Queensland Press, St Lucia, Qld, 1983), p. 40. According to Robert Macklin, in his *Fire in the Blood: The epic tale of Frank Gardiner and others* (Allen & Unwin, Sydney, 2005), Gardiner's stepfather Henry Monro was the expelled son of a professor of medicine at Edinburgh University, Alexander Monro, the last of three generations all with the same name and the same status. It is not impossible that Frank Gardiner benefited somewhat from that connection.

14 'Gardner again', *Sydney Morning Herald*, 17 May 1862, p. 4. The misspelling of Gardiner's name was not uncommon at the time; whereas the occasional reference to 'Sir W. F. Pottinger' in Gardiner's published letters seems to have been a deliberate slight.

15 See Burrangong correspondent, *Empire*, 6 December 1861, p. 3.

X. THE ILL-TEMPERED CAVALIER

1 This in an age innocent of drugs. Significantly, not a Jackie (W.H. Pinkstone, *Early Colonial Days: The biography of a reliable old native, John McGuire,* Eugowra Promotion and Progress Association, Orange, NSW, 2009, p. 62).

2 Shiel, *Ben Hall, Bushranger*, p. 103.

3 Billy Dargan was the tracker who found Ben Hall, and, according to John McGuire, was actually the first to shoot the sleeping bushranger; see Pinkstone, *Early Colonial Days*, p. 104. A summary account of Dargan's activity and accomplishment can be found in Michael Bennett, *Pathfinders: A history of Aboriginal trackers in New South Wales* (NewSouth Books, Kensington, NSW, 2020, pp. 36–44).

4 This according to Julie V. Arbalis, *A Local History of Tarago and Lake Bathurst*, The Author, Canberra, 2006, p. 26. She recounts a preliminary meeting between a number of the leading figures in the forthcoming Eugowra robbery, and a subordinate cast as well, who became restive and that ended fatally for one of them. But she added the Clarke

brothers to this rogue's gallery, somewhat ahead of their actual activity; and she has Ben Hall on his return home involved in shooting Constable Sam Nelson at Collector, though that event did not take place until some years later. However, she does name the horse.

5 Cited in Shiel, *Ben Hall, Bushranger*, p. 52.

6 Kathie Tisdell, *Ben Hall, the Highwayman*, Forbes Shire Council, Forbes, NSW, 2012, p. 284.

7 To preserve the reader's steady concentration on the matter of this book, you can find the relevant passage in Canto 1 (of course, for who reads beyond that?) of *Don Juan*, stanzas 133–89. Indeed, it is a salutary revelation to see evidence here that young ladies of sufficient taste would present the likes of Sir Frederick with a volume of Byron.

8 Hay, which was his first choice, was formerly called Lang's Crossing; the other possible crossing place was Narrandera.

9 See Alec Morrison, *Frank Gardiner: Bushranger to businessman (1830 to 1904)*, Wiley, Milton, Qld, 2003, p. 92.

10 ibid., p. 93.

11 *Border Post, 'Gardinerism and its origins'*, cited in *Yass Courier*, 3 September 1862, p. 3.

12 *Empire*, 27 June 1862, p. 8. The reference is to Gottfried Bürger's 'Die Wilde Jäger', translated by Sir Walter Scott as 'The Wild Hunter', and the source of numerous gothic illustrations. Those who are reading with sympathetic attention will notice here the cunning reappearance of the bandicoot, emerging as a motif in the Germanic manner.

XI. PLAYING WITH FIRE

1 A report some time after the event reveals that Frank Gardiner may already have been inside the cabin, and emerged at about 3 am, and was walking his horse towards the scrub when Sir Frederick called on him to stand. That may be more satisfying to the reader of romances; it hardly changes the confrontation and its outcome – only the direction of the horse; see *Freeman's Journal*, 'Sir Frederick Pottinger's interview with Gardiner', 1 October 1862, p. 3, and copied from the *Goulburn Chronicle*. Pottinger's report, reprinted in James Phelps, *Australian Heist* (Melbourne, Harper Collins, 2018, pp. 101–2), says that Gardiner

was coming towards the hut, cantering rather than walking. He says Pottinger pointed his carbine across the horse's shoulder – he was that close. But of course Pottinger might have preferred to say that Gardiner was coming rather than going, because if Gardiner were inside all the while, the police had been remiss in waiting rather than attacking. That would have done nothing for their reputation. His report also spells out that two persons could be seen to have been sleeping in the four-poster bed; he saw the remnants of supper, a bottle of gin and a box of revolver caps; so Gardiner had been there after all? Pottinger cannot have it both ways.

2 *Burrangong Courier*, 27 August 1862.

3 'The bloody field of Wheogo', *Sydney Morning Herald*, 23 August 1862, p. 5.

4 Cited in Morrison, *Frank Gardiner*, p. 104.

5 ibid., p. 103.

6 'Bathurst Police Court: Mocket v Pottinger', *Bell's Life in Sydney and Sporting Review*, 4 October 1862, p. 3.

7 Superintendent Edric Morisset, born on Norfolk Island, where his father was commandant of the prison colony. He was almost the same age as Freddy, and looked very much like him too.

8 *Empire*, 12 February 1863, p. 4.

9 'Sticking-up the police station at the Pinnacle, on the Lachlan Road', *Yass Courier*, 18 February 1863, p. 2. Other accounts suggest breakfast had nothing to do with the matter. The officer in charge and one other trooper had gone to Forbes, leaving another trooper in attendance. He had been temporarily absent when the station was broken into. A tracker was quick to catch up with them, Ben Hall and another, Patsy Daley; and the usual excited but harmless exchange of shots, misfiring guns etc. followed.

10 'The Lachlan Gold Fields', *Bell's Life in Sydney and Sporting Chronicle*, 7 March 1863, p. 3.

11 Pinkstone, *Early Colonial Days*, p. 92.

12 Shiel proposes that this action had occurred the previous year, 10 August, just before Ben Hall's release. That would put his action the night after he missed shooting Frank Gardiner, and constructs a different narrative

altogether. The difficulty with this timing is that Pottinger claimed in his report that he had given the women in question three days notice of their eviction; and that he had authorisation from the then current owner though he never produced this authority. Pottinger's claim that Hall was one of the greatest villains in the country – a sentiment echoed by the Premier – was well in advance of any supporting evidence. Shiel himself agrees that to claim this as justification for burning the hut is 'demonstrably false' (p. 62). And the local newspapers are astonishingly silent at that time about the hostility of the police action; see Shiel, *Ben Hall, Bushranger*, pp. 61–5. But worst of all, for Shiel, is that Pottinger himself defends his action in a report to the government in July 1863; see *Sydney Morning Herald*, 16 July 1863, p. 4. Curiously, John McGuire – who was Ben Hall's original partner in the property, and whose wife was one of the two women living in the hut – neglects to make any mention of the burning-down of that property in Pinkstone's *Early Colonial Days*.

13 *Sydney Morning Herald*, 16 July 1863, p. 4; Shiel, *Ben Hall, Bushranger*, p. 122.

14 Charles MacAlister, *Old Pioneering Days in the Sunny South*, Chas. MacAlister Book Publication Committee, Goulburn, 1907, p. 259: 'Sir Fred. Pottinger's effigy, worked in straw, was burned in the street one night amid the execrations of 5000 citizens, to mark the low state into which Pottinger had fallen in the opinion of the community.'

XII. KICKING AGAINST THE PRICKS

1 *Courier* (Brisbane), 28 April 1863, p. 3.

2 Charles Harpur, *The Bushrangers: A play in five acts, and other poems*, W.R. Piddington, Sydney, 1853; one of those literary performances more honoured in the breach than in the observance, perhaps.

3 Report of Parliamentary debate, *Empire*, 17 July 1863, p. 5.

4 *Yass Courier*, 25 July 1865.

5 *Yass Chronicle*, 1 August 1863, p. 2.

6 *Empire*, 6 June 1863, p. 5.

7 There is some doubt about who actually shot him. Quite possibly Ben Hall, whose history of accidents and misses almost matches Freddy Pottinger's; see Shiel, *Ben Hall, Bushranger*, p. 166.

8 'The Bushrangers near Eugowra', *Bell's Life*, 14 November 1863, p. 3.

9 *Leader* (Melbourne), 21 November 1863, p. 1.

10 'The bushrangers at Canowindra', *Sydney Morning Herald*, 13 November 1863, p. 5. Compare the slightly blunter wording in the report in *Yass Courier*, 25 November 1863, p. 2.

11 *Yass Courier*, 25 November 1863, p. 2.

12 *Freeman's Journal*, 22 December 1863, p. 3.

XIII. THE SILLY SEASON

1 William Shakespeare, *Henry IV, Part 1*, act 4, line 3.

2 Shiel, *Ben Hall, Bushranger*, p. 133.

3 Pinkstone, *Early Colonial Days*, p. 90.

4 *Sydney Morning Herald*, 2 May 1864, p. 5.

5 Shiel, *Ben Hall, Bushranger*, p. 160.

6 'Ben Hall's gang at Bang Bang', from the *Burrangong Star's* correspondent, *Sydney Morning Herald*, 3 June 1864, p. 5. It would be safe to assume 'wretch' was a modest approximation. Much likelier would have been an adverse reflection on the officer's legitimacy.

7 'General news: bushranging', *Illawarra Mercury*, 31 May 1864, p. 2.

8 Shiel, *Ben Hall, Bushranger*, p. 172.

9 'Ben Hall and his gang', *Sydney Morning Herald*, 18 August 1864, p. 5.

10 *Sydney Morning Herald*, 25 June 1864, p. 7.

11 *Sydney Morning Herald*, 19 August 1864, p. 5.

12 Shiel, *Ben Hall, Bushranger*, p. 106.

13 ibid.

14 *Sydney Punch*, 27 August 1864, p. 4.

15 *New South Wales Police Gazette*, 31 August 1864, p. 273. His name was James McPherson but for the duration in New South Wales he let himself be known as John Bruce.

16 P.W. McNally, *The Life and Adventures of the Wild Scotchman: The Queensland bushranger*, Outridge Printing, Brisbane, 1899, p. 6.

17 'A day with Ben Hall and his gang', *Young Tribune*, 17 December 1864, repr., *Sydney Morning Herald*, 21 December 1864, p. 13.

18 *Bell's Life in Sydney and Sporting Review*, 1 October 1864, p. 3.

19 For example, *Empire*, 26 December, 1864, p. 1.

XIV. THE FINISHING POST

1 John O'Sullivan, *Mounted Police in NSW*, Rigby, Adelaide, 1979, p. 100. In the same place O'Sullivan also sets down quite confidently that Freddy was on his way to bankruptcy. The *Sydney Morning Herald* (21 March 1865) commented that 'For the benefit of the people of Sydney and the other larger towns it may be well to explain that the so-called Wowingragong racecourse differs in no respect from the surrounding open bush', cited in Tisdell, *Ben Hall, the Highwayman*, p. 254.

2 Edward Taylor, 'First racing at Forbes: some historic matches', *Forbes Advocate*, 23 September 1921, p. 9. At the inaugural race meeting there, in 1862, 16 drinking booths had been decided by public auction; and Sir Frederick Pottinger was one of the stewards; see Tisdell, *Ben Hall, the Highwayman*, p. 219.

3 ibid.

4 *Yass Courier*, 14 January 1865, p. 2.

5 'Town talk and table chat', *Herald* (Melbourne), 31 January 1865, p. 2.

6 'Ben Hall's gang', *Empire*, 17 January 1865, p. 8, copying from the Forbes correspondent of the *Orange Guardian*.

7 'Sir Frederick Pottinger: old Forbes days', by 'Old Chum' (in the Sydney *Truth*), *Forbes Advocate*, 2 April 1912, p. 3; J.C.L. Fitzpatrick, *Those Were the Days* (NSW Bookstall Co., Sydney, 1923, p. 127), drawing on the same the authority of the same colourful racing identity, Dan Mayne, remembers differently: Sir Frederick borrowed a horse, Volunteer. It wasn't up to scratch either.

8 There might be a more immediate, less romantic, explanation: one of the early characters in Forbes was 'Scrammy Jack' Monahan from Bendigo, a one-armed man wonderfully smart both at billiards and as a coach driver and trader (MacAlister, *Old Pioneering Days in the Sunny South*, p. 257).

9 'Town talk and table chat', *Herald* (Melbourne), 31 January 1865, p. 2.

10 Fitzpatrick, *Those Were the Days*, p. 126.

11 ibid., p. 125.

12 Quoted in Shiel, *Ben Hall, Bushranger*, p. 52.

13 Selth, 'A splendid type of the genuine English gentleman', p. 38.

14 Fitzpatrick, *Those Were the Days*, p. 124.

15 Shiel, *Ben Hall, Bushranger*, p. 52.
16 George Pottinger, *Sir Henry Pottinger*, p. 164.
17 Selth, 'A splendid type of the genuine English gentleman', p. 40.
18 'Caught at last', *Empire*, 23 February 1865, p. 4.
19 Fitzgerald, *Those Were the Days*, p. 127.
20 *Empire*, 7 March 1865, p. 4.
21 https://www.australianpolice.com.au/frederick-william-pottinger.
22 George Pottinger, *Sir Henry Pottinger*, p. 164. The source he relies on is that authoritative publication, the *Australian Daily Mirror*, April–May 1949. The date of the publication hardly reassures us of its credibility.
23 Another considerable expenditure emerged after his death too: he had owned another racehorse, named (provocatively) Goldfinger, but it had been taken by Ben Hall and his gang (noted in the *Queanbeyan Age*, 4 May 1865), which would have been a further spur to the antipathy Freddy had for his arch foe.

DÉJÀ VU

1 *Sydney Morning Herald*, 23 August 1862, p. 5. An article in the *Forbes Advocate* (2 April 1912, p. 3) and copied from the Sydney *Truth*, confidently attributes the poem to G.B. Barton, elder brother of Sir Edmund ('Toby') Barton. The pseudonymical address is at odds with his movements. Barton had not long returned to Sydney from London; he had been called to the Bar in 1860. On the other hand, a year or two afterwards he became editor of the Sydney *Punch*.
2 *Bell's Life in Sydney and Sporting Chronicle*, 23 August 1862, p. 2.
3 *Albury Banner and Wodonga Express*, 6 September 1862, p. 4.
4 Australian version of traditional folksong, used by the Drunken Poachers in the film *The Legend of Ben Hall* (2016).

Wakefield Press is an independent publishing and distribution company based in Adelaide, South Australia. We love good stories and publish beautiful books. To see our full range of books, please visit our website at www.wakefieldpress.com.au where all titles are available for purchase. To keep up with our latest releases and news, subscribe to the *Wakefield Weekly* at https://mailchi.mp/wakefieldpress/subscribe

Find us!

Facebook: www.facebook.com/wakefield.press
Instagram: www.instagram.com/wakefieldpress

www.ingramcontent.com/pod-product-compliance
Lightning Source LLC
La Vergne TN
LVHW030914080826
845145LV00012B/2889

* 9 7 8 1 9 2 3 3 8 8 6 6 6 *